Hell and Salvation

HELL and
SALVATION

Leslie H. Woodson

FLEMING H. REVELL COMPANY
Old Tappan, New Jersey

Library of Congress Cataloging in Publication Data

Woodson, Leslie H ⸺, date
   Hell and salvation.

   Bibliography: p.
   1. Hell. I. Title.
BT836.2.W6   236'.25   72-10942
ISBN 0-8007-0581-5

Contents

Foreword by Robert E. Coleman   9

Introduction   11

1   *Gehenna, Hades, Tartarus*—Scriptural Word Study   17

2   Interpretations of Hell   29

3   Eternal Punishment?   41

4   Conditional Immortality?   49

5   Universalism—Will All Be Saved?   55

6   The Nature of God   65

7   Hell—A Motivating Force in Evangelism   75

8   Today's Evangelism and the Forgotten Concept   85

9   The Essence of Hell   103

10 If I Go to Hell . . . . (A Sermon)   109

Bibliography   119

Index   125

Foreword

Walter Hooper once told C. S. Lewis that he knew of a headstone, on which the epitaph read, "Here lies an atheist, all dressed up but with nowhere to go." Whereupon the famous author replied, "I bet he wishes that were so."

In a sense, everyone wishes it were so. Who can find delight in the realization that persons who scorn God must face the prospect of an eternal hell? Certainly, the Christian finds no pleasure in the judgment of the wicked. As with our Lord, the contemplation of what it means for a soul to be lost can bring nothing but tears to the heart.

But it is still a fact with which we must reckon. However painful, there can be no evasion of the subject if we are to take seriously the teachings of Christ.

For this reason, we can be grateful for this forthright treatment of a doctrine too often ignored by modern churchmen. The author is not afraid to face the witness of Scripture. Yet he is not unmindful of points of view different from his own. Other interpretations and their implications are considered with the scholar's objectivity. Throughout there is a refreshing evangelical realism in his perspective.

Reading these pages should make us more aware of God's grace. Surely it is His desire that none should perish. Jesus has made a Way through the cross by which all who come to Him may be saved. The choice is ours. And as we cannot avoid that decision, so we cannot escape its ultimate consequences.

ROBERT E. COLEMAN

Introduction

Of particular concern to those who stand squarely in the midstream of scriptural Christianity is the growing confusion which prevails like a heavy fog in the Christian world. The entire problem appears to stem from a developing tendency to discredit the Bible as the inspired and authoritative Word of God. Unless one derives his faith from the Scriptures of the Judeo-Christian community he will have no recourse other than to substitute one of the man-centered theologies of his time. All such systems of belief are attempts to understand and explain the meaning of life on the premises of humanistic philosophy. Either we settle on the written Word of God as objective truth revealed to the world by God Himself or we get caught up in a maze of uninspired meanderings through endless theological debates. The shambles in which modern theology finds itself is almost totally responsible for the strange and outlandish beliefs, or lack of them, found among the confused members of a typical church.

Theological innovations have assumed the appearance of a variety of trinkets displayed in a novelty shop. They attract us by their seeming originality, their clever design. We are prone to ask about much of the "new theology." We hear customers browsing in those novelty shops say, "Wonder who thought up that cute idea?" There are so many ideas being circulated as gospel truth that men and women without a thorough acquaintance with the Biblical narrative are left in a quandary to make decisions purely on the basis of which current theory is in vogue or sounds more rational. Man's belief is determined cafeteria-style so that the modern church member picks and chooses that which is most palatable for him. The trouble with such a method of determining what we shall believe is that, without a norm by which to check our ideas, truth becomes completely subjective and relative. There is no objective criterion for judgment and no absolute, "Thus saith the Lord!"

In the wake of the contemporary theological hash being served in every medium of communication, there is more and more tolerance for a multiplicity of non-Biblical concepts and less and less tolerance for any absolutism found in the Word itself. Some are voicing the opinion that doctrines are divisive and hamper the progress of the church. Biblical theology gives place to relational theology where man discards his doctrinal stance in deference to a more flexible religious faith by which he can *relate* to his fellows. In true Christianity there is no conflict between doctrine and relationships. To sacrifice either for the other would suggest that something is askew in our discipleship.

Nowhere is the ambiguity about Biblical doctrine more readily seen than in the light-hearted way in which the concept of hell is treated. The idea was of paramount interest to the church during former days of its history. Today the word has all but disappeared from the vocabulary of modern churchmen. If it is mentioned at all, it is either done in senseless profanity or thoughtless jesting. For some the word has become padding for an inadequate vocabulary—enforcement for ineffective communication. For others, it serves as a subject for a good joke which creates a devil-may-care impression among persons who subconsciously feel that they have cut the nerve of hell by making fun of it. Other than this usage of the term, the concept has long since been abandoned by the average church member. Hardly anyone would insult another by presuming that hell is a final possibility for any human being. Clergymen are especially hesitant to mention the word for fear of being called *fundamentalist* or something worse.

A statement by the late Bishop James Pike is used by Will Oursler in a recent book to give a cross section of views on heaven and hell:

A Heaven of infinite bliss and a Hell of infinite torment is an impossible contradiction. The kind of people who would qualify for heaven would not be in bliss knowing that there were a lot of people in suffering with no chance whatever for change—the have-nots, the underprivileged. These suitable for Heaven would want to go to Hell to be alongside them in their needs. Jesus, as shown by the reports of his ministry on earth, would be there alongside them too. God in his heaven would find himself lonely and might well join everybody there—or change the whole scheme.—WILL OURSLER, *Protestant Power and the Coming Revolution*, p. 173

Of natural consequence, therefore, it is expedient that one should ask what place the ancient concept has in the contemporary message. Are we justified in our almost total neglect of the idea? Did Jesus actually teach that some will be eternally lost and punished in an everlasting hell? If so, dare we ignore this aspect of our teaching? If not, how did the New Testament happen to include the concept as an integral part of the preaching and teaching of Christ? These are questions which haunt the mind of the serious student of eschatology (study of the end times) as it relates to the redemptive mission of the church.

Churchmen who hold to any validity at all in the doctrine of hell believe in one of these three interpretations: those who hold the view of an endless existence of punishment for evil, those who insist on a less severe and remedial circumstance of judgment, and those who advocate sudden and irrevocable annihilation.

It shall be the purpose of this book to investigate the use and meaning of the New Testament idea of *gehenna* (hell), to make an accurate study of the word itself as it was understood by those who employed the term in the writing of the New Testament record. It shall further be our objective to show how this concept has developed and broadened to include the three interpretations stated above. The concluding portion of the book shall be dedicated to an investigation of how the concept is being used in the mission of the church today and in what additional manner it might possibly be utilized. As a last chapter we have added a sample sermon which it is hoped will serve as a challenge to pastors to deal more openly with the theme. It is further antici-pated that the sermon will help fill the doctrinal void for laymen who often have not been given the whole picture.

Extensive research in available theological and Biblical writ-ings will comprise the foundation and much of the building materials for that which is to follow. The writer shall not be averse to using commentary sources where it is believed that they will be helpful in throwing additional light on the subject. In every instance, the material will be documented in order that credit may be given and that readers may know where to look for addi-tional help. Each source has been given at the end of the quota-tion to make reading easier, and bibliographical information is included at the end of the book. It is not our intention to add to the present store of knowledge in the field, but to uncover possi-bilities and present an unbiased coverage of the facts as we un-derstand them.

Discussion questions are included at the end of each chapter so that the reader may—either individually or in a study group—explore his knowledge and understanding of this long-neglected subject. Not all the works included in the bibliography at the back of this book deal exclusively with hell, but each one of them has some content matter which relates to the topic under study.

This book has been written in the conviction that an evangelical perspective on hell is long overdue in the modern church, and with a prayer that it will restore a Biblical truth to the prominent place reserved for it on the pages of the New Testament.

Hell and Salvation

1

Gehenna, Hades, Tartarus– Scriptural Word Study

Gehenna is one of three New Testament words which have been rendered into English by the term *hell*. The other two words are *hades* and *tartarus*. Contemporary translators of the Scriptures have taken advantage of the findings of Biblical scholarship in distinguishing between the three Greek terms and rendering only *gehenna* as hell. *Hades,* identified with the Hebrew *sheol,* is better carried over into English by transliteration (equivalent word sound) than by translation (identical or similar meaning with different phonetic sound). It refers to the place of the departed dead, the underworld, and actually means that which is *unseen* (Matthew 11:23; 16:18; Luke 10:15; 16:23; Acts 2:27, 31; Revelation 1:18; 6:8; 20:13, 14). *Tartarus* is used only once in the New Testament in 2 Peter 2:4 and is identified with the place especially reserved for fallen angels. This word is also more correctly rendered without translation.

It is of interest to note that *gehenna* is itself a transliteration into Greek of the Hebrew *Gehinnom* (valley of Hinnom) where children were burnt to Moloch in the days of Kings Ahaz and Manasseh. Jeremiah prophesies against the wickedness of the sons of Judah who had "built the high place of Topheth, which is in the valley of the son of Hinnom, to burn their sons and their daughters in the fire; which I did not command, nor did it come into my mind" (Jeremiah 7:31 rsv). Desecrated in the time of King Josiah, the area was turned into a rubbish heap where the fire burned continually.

The valley was a place of nauseous stench and was recognized as a filthy and polluted parcel of land where nothing of any value could be found. Everything there had been destined for destruction and nothing was worth the effort to redeem it. Thus the "city dump" came to be identified in the Jewish mind as a perfect symbol of the final rejection of wickedness by God and the irrevocable destiny of the wicked themselves. Still today the word hell conjures up such strong images that the hot smell clings to our nostrils.

Enoch (in the apocryphal writings) speaks of a twofold fiery abyss for the impious after death (Enoch 90:20–27). The Apocalypse of Baruch makes a distinction between lesser torment before final judgment and greater punishment after it (Apocalypse of 2 Baruch 36:11). According to the historian, Josephus, the Pharisees moved the place of torment to Hades under the earth (*Antiquities,* XVIII; 1, 3). The idea of a judgment place in *Gehinnom* was never fully given up, only the locality was differently fixed. In the eschatology (view of things to happen at the end of the age) of the Hebrews' *gehenna* was the realm beneath the earth (though somehow more vastly enlarged than space would permit) where the wicked are roasted in fire and gnawed upon by vermin immediately after their deaths. Milton suggests that hell is worse than even the Jews could imagine. He describes it as

> A Universe of death, which God by curse
> Created evil, for evil only good,
> Where all life dies, death lives, and Nature breeds,
> Perverse, all monstrous, all prodigious things,
> Abominable, inutterable, and worse
> Than Fables yet have feign'd, or fear conceiv'd.
> *Paradise Lost,* II, 622–28

This concept was prevalent in the time of Jesus and the preaching of the New Testament Church.

The word *hell* is found only twelve times in the entire New Testament. Eleven of these uses are in the Synoptic Gospels (Matthew 5:22, 29, 30; 10:28; 18:9; 23:15, 33; Mark 9:43, 45, 47; Luke 12:5). The other appearance of the word is in James 3:6 where hell is described as the source of injury done by an evil and malicious tongue. It is interesting to note that Paul does not use the concept of hell or apocalyptic phrases associated with it. The same observation may be made about the writings of John. It should be observed, however, that while the author of Revelation (the writer accepts the traditional view of Johannine authorship for the Apocalypse) does not use the word itself, he does employ numerous terms descriptive of hell. The *lake of fire* (Revelation 19:20; 20:10, 14, 15; 21:8) is an example. There is general agreement that this fiery lake is to be identified as similar, if not equivalent, to the Hebrew *gehenna* or the Greek hell. It is a place of final damnation for the rebels against God. The Pauline and general epistles also make several references to the idea incorporated in hell without ever using the word (Philippians 3:19; 2 Thessalonians 1:9; Hebrews 10:39; 2 Peter 2:17; Jude 13).

In each instance where the word *hell* is used in the Synoptics it is employed by Jesus Himself. If for no other reason than this we are enjoined to take seriously the concept of the term and the context in which it is used. Matthew records the word seven times, Mark three times, and Luke once. Some have reasoned from Matthew's larger use of hell that he has increased the stress which Jesus placed on the concept. It is often assumed that Matthew draws his material from the book of Enoch and that both writers owe their form to an unknown but shared imaginative tradition. There are always those who insist that the details surrounding the idea of hell are too meager to warrant any doctrine other than that Jesus did warn men to repent and follow Him. On the contrary, it would seem that some specific details are at least inferred by the Master in the statements which He makes in these eleven choice excerpts.

If the date of writing given to the gospels is correct, Mark records earlier than either Matthew or Luke the fearful words of

Jesus relating to the wisdom with which one parts with his
physical members as compared to the folly which allows one's
whole life to be lost in hell. The first narrator remembers (as
does Matthew later in 5:29, 30; 18:8, 9) having been instructed
by Simon Peter to write down the words of the Lord.

> And if your hand causes you to sin, cut it off; it is better for
> you to enter life maimed than with two hands to go to hell,
> to the unquenchable fire. And if your foot causes you to sin,
> cut it off; it is better for you to enter life lame than with
> two feet to be thrown into hell. And if your eye causes you
> to sin, pluck it out; it is better for you to enter the king-
> dom of God with one eye than with two eyes to be thrown
> into hell, where their worm does not die, and the fire is not
> quenched.—Mark 9:43–48 RSV

It will be noted that verses 44 and 46 are not found in some of
the later translations. They are not in the earliest Greek manu-
scripts but are identical with verse 48 which is genuine. It can
hardly be doubted that the substance of the saying goes back to
Jesus Himself.

Some are unimpressed by the fact that Jesus is reported to
have made these statements about hell. For such persons the
basic picture of Jesus given in the New Testament is that of a
kind, sympathetic, compassionate spirit. Thus any harsh words
of judgment and condemnation from His lips seem out of place
and foreign to His nature. The higher critics insist that a distinction must be made between what is commonly referred to as the
old tradition and ideas produced in and by the church. Added
to this is the matter of the narrators themselves having edited
what they wrote. The difficulty with this kind of Biblical criticism
is that it is almost purely subjective. Deletions depend on one's
opinion and once the scissors are used there seems to be no
stopping place for the average critic. *Evidence is sufficient for
the belief that Jesus shared the idea of a fiery hell for the wicked.*

Right in the middle of the Sermon on the Mount Jesus has
some severe words about hell and its threat to man. ". . . whoever says, 'You fool!' shall be liable to the hell of fire" (Matthew

5:22 rsv). The New English Bible puts it: ". . . if he sneers at him [his brother] he will have to answer for it in the fires of hell." Here the sin is failure to recognize any good at all in another and the assumption of a place of accusation and judgment which belongs to God alone. When *hell* is coupled with the additional description of *fire*, it seems clear that Jesus was thinking of the fire which burned eternally in hell and offered the most abhorrent, characteristic symbol of being refused by the Eternal. Here Christ goes beyond the law against murder and equates uncontrolled and malicious anger with killing itself. Killing is not done alone with knives and guns, but with contemptuous attitudes and caustic accusations against another's character. The word *hell* is, therefore, not too strong to apply here.

In the tenth chapter of Matthew, Jesus warns, "and do not fear those who kill the body but cannot kill the soul; rather fear him who can destroy both soul and body in hell" (Matthew 10:28 rsv). While there is some debate as to whether it is God or Satan who destroys, there is no question about the fear motivation arising from the thought of hell, a low level but effective motivation for doing right. Hell is deliberately joined to the final judgment upon sin as designed by the Eternal God. The evangelist Luke records a similar saying of the Lord (Luke 12:5).

The remaining reference to hell is again found in Matthew at the point where Christ pronounces His sevenfold woe upon the Pharisees.

> Woe to you, scribes and Pharisees, hypocrites! for you traverse sea and land to make a single proselyte and when he becomes a proselyte, you make him twice as much a child of hell as yourselves. . . . You serpents, you brood of vipers, how are you to escape being sentenced to hell?
> —Matthew 23:15, 33 rsv

The interesting expression, "the child of hell," is a Hebraism for an extremely rebellious and totally wicked person. In both the above denunciations in Matthew 23 the Lord emphatically denies the possibility of escaping the final judgment and its sen-

tence of hell to those whose attitudes and actions involve others
in their own "hellishness."

In view of the composite scholarship surrounding the use of
the term under study in the years of our Lord and the period
immediately following in the Ancient Church, only one conclusion can be drawn by the writer. Though there have been variations in emphasis on the concept of hell from the beginning, the
idea which surrounds the term as it was used in the days of
Jesus is that of final damnation and unutterable anguish for the
wicked. When Jesus used the term, it was always in that sense.
The apostles followed the popular concept in their writings
primarily because Jesus endorsed it. We can be certain that they
never would have done so if there had been any hint from their
Lord that the idea of final and eternal doom for the wicked was
not correct. And we can be further sure that Jesus would have
been especially careful to condemn so important an idea if it
had been untrue.

Our word study would not be complete without some con-
sideration of the bearing of a pre-Copernican view upon the concept. We are cautioned by Biblical scholars against retaining the
cosmology (view of the universe) of the people of Jesus' time
in a period when science has disproved the three-decker universe
theory. The ancients believed that the earth was at the center
of everything, that it was flat with an area "down under" and an
area above the surface which was shaped like a huge dome. The
Lord dwelt somewhere beyond the visible dome and the devil
lived gnomelike somewhere beneath the terra firma. At death
the righteous, who were buried in the soil, would eventually go
to live with God above the dome. By the same token, the wicked
would descend into *hades* where they would be tormented by
the devil. While the Hebrew concept of developments in the
world to come was not a full-blown doctrine, it was not so form-
less as to leave the Jews without some notion about the general
state and place of the good and bad after death.

Copernicus was to put an end to the three-decker idea. Space
was to take on an entirely new meaning and the universe was
destined to be seen in a completely new perspective. No longer

could the earth be construed as the center of everything. Rather it was to be observed as only one of many such land masses revolving around the sun. Up was no longer *really* up and down was no longer *really* down. While the scientist was not particularly concerned with religious theories it was inevitable that such findings would have a direct and significant bearing on the views of the church. With this in mind there is little surprise when we find the church of the sixteenth century rebelling against the views of the so-called atheistic scientists.

In this space age, which is accelerating with incredible speed in its discovery of broadening horizons, man probes deeper into outer space without finding either God or His heaven. Of course, one would be naïve indeed if he actually expected to discover a spiritual realm in a material dimension. It seems to be an assumed and accepted fact, nonetheless, that if man finds no evidence of "heaven" in space there is likewise no "hell" located in the opposite direction. This whole logic undercuts practically every aspect of the Christian faith. It alters our idea of God in the *heights* so that theologians can now refer to God as "the Ground of being" found in the *depths* of man's existence. Either way, as can easily be observed, God is still caricatured as a spatial figure. In keeping with this rationale (which has many such weaknesses) the world of the supranatural is explained away and Rudolph Bultmann's demythologizing paves the way for Paul Tillich, Teilhard de Chardin, James Pike, and John Robinson.

One of the interesting inconsistencies in the modern rebellion against Biblical cosmology is the widespread assumption that the new view is scientific. On the one hand we are told that man has long since learned that the earth is not the center of the universe. Rather the earth is dependent on the sun for its very life. It literally exists in an orbit which is controlled by the sun's power. This is an acknowledgement that there is something at the heart of the universe which is more important than this little world of ours. On the other hand, we have not yet learned that the human species which thrives on this earth is not the reason for which all else exists. We still proudly assert ourselves and mount our little self-made throne in a repudiation of a divine and sovereign Creator-Redeemer who dwells at the center and before whom man is responsible. If the sun rather than the earth is the center it is reasonable to suspect that God rather than man is the pivot around which we have our being. Thus we are in no position to make pronouncements which either annul or restrict the supranatural.

We are not simply being asked to abandon an obsolete cosmology but we are expected to adopt a world view which is constructed on a purely naturalistic assumption. No room is to be left for divine revelation. What man cannot explain is unacceptable. Everything must fit into our scientific molds. Religion must fit into the scientific system, and more—it must *ultimately* become a science. There is no longer any room for mystery or faith. Heaven and hell cannot be even seriously considered as symbols since symbols represent reality and the new cosmology has put an end to both otherworld concepts. Bultmann can write:

> Man's knowledge and mastery of the world have advanced to such an extent through science and technology that it is no longer possible for anyone seriously to hold the New Testament view of the world—in fact, there is no one who does. . . . No one who is old enough to think for himself supposes that God lives in a local heaven. There is no longer any heaven in the traditional sense of the word. The same applies to hell in the sense of a mythical underworld beneath our feet. . . . —*Kerygma and Myth,* p. 4

The secular mind-set leaves little room for disagreement because it is almost "religiously" affirmed that no truth can exist outside the scientific orb. What is so often overlooked is that there are different truth dimensions and truth in one of these dimensions need not be denied by truth in another. Their natures are not the same. Thus, one can be intellectually honest while embracing both a Copernican view of the physical world and a three-decker view of the metaphysical world at one and the same time.

It probably needs to be considered that the people of our Lord's time who spoke in terms of heaven *above* and hell *below* were using current and popular terminology to refer to something too mysterious to describe otherwise. We can easily reflect upon our own scientific superiority by attempting to put the people of an earlier period of time into a straitjacket which they might reject were they able to defend their science or explain their theology.

A contemporary scholar, though in another context, writes words which may shed some light on the whole realm of cosmology.

> Moreover, is the Bible to be berated as "scientifically inaccurate" because the sacred writers employed terms which were in common use at the time, and which in many instances are still in daily idiomatic use in our own scientifically enlightened day? Is it such a scientific blunder to say the "sun rose" or the "sun set" (Ecclesiastes 1:5) or the "dew fell" (Numbers 11:9) when we all constantly say so in a day when every schoolboy knows that the sun does not rotate around the earth, but the earth rotates on its own axis and also around the sun, and that the dew does not "fall"? Are the hagiographers to be mocked as fools or commended for their common sense in delivering a popular account and accommodating themselves to the environment and intelligence of their audience?—MERRILL F. UNGER, *Introductory Guide to the Old Testament*, pp. 39, 40

A contemporary author who holds ten academic degrees in science, psychology, philosophy, and religion affirms this use of ancient symbolism in a vein similar to the above quote from Unger.

> We talk about the sun rising in the morning and setting in the evening. We have a particular meaning in mind and do not intend by this to be making scientific statements about the motion of the sun. Can we expect them in ancient times to be any different?—JAMES H. JAUNCEY, *Science Returns to God*, p. 29

The common people still talk about heaven as *up* and hell as *down*. Obviously, this is not just a hangover from an unenlightened day when men were scientifically uninformed. Rather is it a built-in symbolism which is observed as well in man's whole system of values which insists on progress being *upward* and failure being *downward*. Life's *higher* values are the better ones and we reach for them. *Lower* values are to be rejected and we flee from them. Where heaven or hell is to be located must remain a mystery whether one's cosmology is that of the first or the twentieth century. It seems to be enough that man has an inner certainty by nature that somewhere the two places of eternal extremes do exist. The symbolism has changed very little in spite of our scientific sophistication and our repudiation of a view of the universe which may have been far more symbolic for the ancients than we are willing to admit.

In this rather limited study of the word *gehenna* (hell) and the bearing which the ancients' view of the universe had upon it, we have sought to establish as fact that the teaching of Jesus was not dissimilar to that of the popular theory of His day. We have further attempted to show that the New Testament does record the sayings of Jesus accurately and that the apostles shared the belief about hell which characterized the ministry of our Lord. Finally, we have sought to deal with the matter of cosmology from both a scientific and a theological perspective. There is no reason, as the writer understands the issues, to deny the existence of hell as both a state of being and a place of habitation in the world to come.

In the following chapters we shall be looking at the manner in which the church has handled the Biblical idea across the centuries. We shall try to look at the varied interpretations in all honesty as they are compared with and balanced by the scriptural account.

Discussion Questions for Chapter 1

1. *Explain the difference between the words* gehenna, hades, *and* tartarus *as used in the Greek New Testament.*

2. *To what was Jesus comparing hell when He referred to it as* gehenna?

3. *How does one account for the neglect of the doctrine of hell in light of the fact that every use of the word in the Synoptics is by Jesus Himself?*

4. *What reason do we have for believing that the Ancient Church has not put words in Jesus' mouth which He did not speak?*

5. *What does the scientific cosmology of our time do to the idea of hell as a "place" of torment? In what way is heaven* up *and* hell down?

6. *To what degree may the ancients be said to have thought in symbols when referring to the world beyond?*

7. *How many of the twelve New Testament references to* gehenna *can you recall? Explain the use of the concept in each one.*

2

Interpretations of Hell

Man in every age is intrigued by the thought of hell and its horrors. He may be able to dismiss lightly the hope of heaven, but there is something haunting about hell. This is why persons who begin a study of Dante find their interest in the Ten Heavens paling into oblivion in comparison to the attraction felt for the vivid description of hell.

While man may be capable of avoiding serious thoughts of life after death, he finds it increasingly difficult to ignore the possibility of *death after life*. The negation of existence is more disturbing to the average man than is the thought of continuous being. And it is quite possible that even those who seek to disprove the theory which insists on life after death are actually attempting another task altogether. Since nothing is built into a man which would create a will to cancel or annul the continuation of improved living, one might logically suggest that the effort to disprove immortality is in reality a disguised desire to repudiate hell. The subconscious suspicion that punishment may follow death can induce a sense of fear in the heart of man which assumes the outward form of hostility toward any kind of postmortem existence.

The contemporary man likes to think of himself as a realist who is not deceived by religious traditions and folklore. Thoughts of heaven and hell after death are pushed aside by the pressures to live *now* as though there is nothing for us but this brief span of earth time. We call this "being realistic." Concern about the world beyond is unworthy of a thinking man. Could it not conceivably be true that a better word than *realists* might be *escapists?* The effort to compensate for the sordid existence of many persons on the earth by anticipating "pie in the sky by and by when we die" may well be an other-wordly escape mechanism. But is the ignoring of final judgment after death by an obsession with the *here* and *now* any less a form of escapism?

The reference to man's hard lot in life as "going through hell" has become so commonplace that the modern mind has satisfied itself with the assumption that hell is nothing more. This is clearly borne out in developing patterns of communication by which we adopt the current motif of speaking of hell in terms of a private or public "hell on earth." Hell is equated with being forced to live in squalor or poverty, struggling through a war, or living with a bad marriage partner.

Hell is where the poor are trapped in a ghetto of indifference. It is the high school campus where some persons are socially crippled because they don't fit. It is the black section of a psychiatric ward at a charity hospital where the bruised ones that didn't get enough love are hidden. It is a small village in Vietnam where people lie in the streets, victims of a stray bomb. It is a dingy jail downtown where frightened human beings cower. It is a small town high school where a teen-age girl returns from a home for unwed mothers after giving birth to her child. It is the street of charred buildings, broken windows, and looted stores— the aftermath of a riot kindled by frustration, hopelessness, and rage.

Hell is the suffering of humanity, the place of man's inhumanity to man. This may not be the only scene in which God calls us to be ambassadors of Christ, but it is clearly one of the most significant. The whole ethic of the Christian life style is to be an agent of love where there is despair; one who cares, where there is little or no caring; a voice for liberation and new life, where there is oppression and hopelessness.

This is the hell to which we are summoned as ambassadors of Christ. Isn't Jesus' vision for a life style the vision of one who goes to the sick, the lost, the poor, the lame, and the oppressed? This journey is held up before us as an option for our lives. Hell is not the place that we usually want to go. But the cry of someone in need is the summons to the hell of our neighbor and to Christ's ministry. . . .
                                    —RON DEVILLIER, *Real*, Spring 1972

We are all quite fully aware of what the above author is saying. And none of us would disagree with him that these situations to which he refers are probably the nearest thing imaginable to "hell on earth." It is quite possible that the author has a much graver concept of hell than this excerpt would suggest. The difficulty is in the overtones, the powers of verbalized suggestion, and the things which are not said. One can easily be left with the impression that this is all there is to hell. Yet, nowhere in either the Old or New Testaments does the Biblical record conceive of hell in this manner. The hell to which the Bible points and against which it warns us is a totally different thing.

Earlier man was obsessed with the fear of confronting the world to come. Contemporary man is afraid to face the world which is already here. While the people of an earlier time saw the present life as rather simple and the life to come as pretty complex, modern man finds today almost impossibly complex and the life to come so simple as to be ignored. Both Dante and Swedenborg think of many hells, the former speaking of *levels* or *circles* and the latter of *quarters*. Dante speaks of Judas as being in the lowest of the ninth circle of hell, while Swedenborg thinks of the worst hells as being in what he calls the "western quarter." Though we cannot be certain, this is probably an intended counterpart to Paul's third heaven (2 Corinthians 12:2) and an attempt to understand degrees of punishment or reward in the world to come.

If man of an earlier age thought in complex fashion of hell, he also sought to communicate his ideas in the most grotesque manner possible. We are literally aghast at some of the pictorial and verbal images conjured up by the fertile minds of artists and writers. A gruesome portrayal of the pangs of hell is found in the Apocryphal New Testament writings of the late second century in which sinners are seen "hanging by their tongues" and "being burned up to their middle . . . and having their entrails devoured by worms that rested not"(Apocalypse of Peter 22–34). Of course, we must admit that this portrayal is basically in agreement with the mental picture which we get from the New Testament.

Hell has been painted with stark crudity as seen in the early twelfth-century mosaic covering the west wall of Torcello Cathedral, near Venice. Christ is seated on the throne between Mary and John while below Him is the Book with the seven seals and to the left are the pitiable souls in hell with the birds and beasts of prey. Even so great a painter as Rubens painted fiends and monsters into his early seventeenth-century scene of the Great Last Judgment. It must be noted that such representations, though honest, were exaggerations of Jesus' reference to the worms of hell and John's beastly symbols in the Apocalypse.

Some of the Early Church fathers did not stop at believing in eternal punishment, but contemplated the fate of the wicked with great joy. Augustine, Aquinas, and Peter Lombard are choice examples. One specific quotation from Aquinas will suffice for the whole.

Wherefore in order that the happiness of the saints may be more delightful to them and that they may render more copious thanks to God for it, they are allowed to see perfectly the sufferings of the damned.—*The Summa Theologica*, XXI, 107

While we must recognize that such speculations came out of periods of great tribulation and persecution, as a general rule, we must also admit that such an attitude is far from Christian. No one who has been snatched from the burning himself can feel anything but compassion and concern for the lost.

About the nearest one can come in modern times to finding

vestigial remains of the coarser portrayal of hell is in the words of Seiss, who himself preached as early as the latter half of the nineteenth century.

> Hell and hell torments are not the mere fictions which some have pronounced them. Neither are they as remote from this present world as men often dream. There is a fiery abyss, with myriads of evil beings in it, malignant and horrible, and there is but a door between this world and that.—*The Apocalypse,* p. 210

This is not to suggest that Seiss would have taken any pleasure in the thought of the punishment of the lost. Far from it. This dedicated Lutheran pastor is remembered as a faithful expositor of the Word of God and a deeply concerned shepherd of the flock. It is rather to suggest that the sternness of earlier days has few spokesmen who so well represent the blunt method of proclamation which characterized the first seventeen centuries of the Christian era. It is possible that, if we can refrain from giving the impression that the punishment of the wicked gives the Christian a feeling of satisfaction, the blunt presentation of the doctrine of hell would be an improvement over our gospel "niceties."

The brightest spots in the preaching of hell in the history of the church have been those occasions when churchmen made neither a capricious judge of God nor deserving victims of sinners. This is not to imply that divine judgment should be lightly treated; nor is it to suggest that man can ever actually deserve anything but hell—otherwise salvation would not be solely a matter of grace. It is rather to say that the concept of hell, at those faithful points in time, has been recognized primarily as the natural outgrowth of man's own choice.

Hell could be an act of divine mercy for the ungodly. If there is anything which would be more unbearable for the wicked than hell, it would have to be heaven. If a man lives his life in utter disregard of God's revealed will for his life, throws out all the restrictions and refuses to be encumbered with moral and ethical restrictions, and makes light of the cross of Christ, it is unthinkable that he could find a trace of happiness in heaven. He would be as completely out of his element as a person allergic to flowers would be if he found himself in the midst of a botanical garden!

Swedenborg was certain that anyone who eventually reaches the habitation of eternal hell will have done so because his strongest love has motivated him in that direction. He insisted that a man's spirit is his ruling love, that is, man is eternally known by the strongest love which motivates his existence. Every man has many loves, but they are akin to and dominated by his sovereign love. All other loves are subservient to that. A logical progression of thought insists that what man loves in this world is simply carried into the next life. There he will continue to love what he has chosen and experience its consequences. Some of those consequences he will already have known to some degree in the present world. But the full force of one's choice is reserved until the final execution of sin's sentence. Judgment is a clarification of and distinction between loves.

Thus we see that some have recognized the necessity of hell, not that God may have a chance to vent His divine spleen and punish the wicked, but that impenitent man may have what he wants. What torment heaven would be for the man who has never loved God or found the least joy in Christian fellowship!

Nonetheless, it must be pointed out that, though hell is the fulfillment of man's choosing, it is not exactly what he expects. We have not been saying that the wicked will be happy with the outcome. What we have said is that the mercy of God will never force anyone to live in heaven when he is not prepared for or acclimated to it.

Dante's genius is awesome as he portrays sinners *at home* in their complementary circle in hell. The punishment reveals, in each instance, the evil man's character. As in reincarnation one observes a swine's body awaiting a "swinish soul," so in the *Inferno* lust is not punished but becomes itself punishment. Passion, for example, is not punished and destroyed, rather it is allowed to become eternally pursued and everlastingly disappointing. That, according to Dante, is hell, indeed.

There is a simple and humorous (though also profoundly sobering) story which has made the rounds but deserves retelling because of its illustrative value.

It seems that a man died and stood before what he surmised was the entrance of heaven. The keeper of the gate advised him that he would be staying within the enclosure forever and assured him as well that anything he requested would be granted. What a joyous thought it was to know that his life had been so well lived that now he could have absolutely anything! He must have done a better job than he had thought.

Everything he had wanted on the earth but had been denied or enjoyed only in limited amounts he began to ask for. Each time his wishes were granted until overindulgence began to make the coveted things unattractive. In fact, life had actually grown a bit monotonous. So he asked for a glance at the old earth planet where he had formerly lived. The sight of war, poverty, injustice, and personal struggle sent him back to his newly-found paradise with new gratitude.

Soon he was more miserable than ever with his lavish surroundings and pampered desires. There was only one thing left that he could think of which he had not enjoyed. Therefore, he asked the keeper to allow him to peep into the pits of hell. And the keeper replied, "And where do you think you are?"

Hell has always been construed as a negative place. Heaven is positive and what heaven is, hell is not. The two places of final destiny are opposing states. That is, hell is the exact opposite of *ouranos* (heaven). The traditional view of the Christian church has been to portray heaven as love, peace, life, joy, and light in unbroken fellowship. Hate, unrest, death, misery, darkness, and gnashing of teeth have been the stock terms for describing hell. Hell has been characterized as "proximity without fellowship" so many times that the original source of the expression is lost. To dwell in an atmosphere of exclusive hostility without the support of God is hell, especially when the place where one dwells is overpopulated with miserable, selfish neighbors. It must be clearly understood that there will be no chance for "jolly good-time fellows" to get together in the nether pits for a grand and glorious spree.

Sartre's *No Exit* is a drama of unredeemed human relationships where hell is other people. Of course, the idea of hell is existential in Sartre, that is, intolerable proximity *here* and *now.* But the eschatological dimension has validity as well. Jesus was far from being ambiguous when He pictured hell as a place where there is weeping and gnashing of teeth (Matthew 8:12; 13:42, 50; 22:13; 24:51; 25:30; Luke 13:28). How could there be anything else in a place where everything is false and corrupt and each man is selfishly at odds with both himself and others?

Another related view of hell which has been propounded since early times is that which insists that hell is to be explained as the remorse of a life of failure. Eustace says to young Sebastian, in Aldous Huxley's *Time Must Have a Stop,* "Hell isn't merely paved with good intentions; it's walled and roofed with them. Yes, and furnished, too." Eternal regrets for a life lived in vain, remorse for evil deeds, and a loathing of oneself for having failed to use the opportunities to do good—that would be hell if there were nothing else. All of us know the inner pathos of failure in this life. We know how useless we feel at such times. But at least we have a chance to correct our past. In hell that last ray of hope will be gone.

The flavor of the centuries is probably caught as well in W. E. Orchard's statement as anywhere:

> If this life does not decide the life to come, then either its purpose is not clear, or it is not properly designed for its purpose; since, if any soul needs a second chance this life might as well have been altogether omitted.—*What Is Hell?*, p. 134

No one could have been more emphatic or unyielding regarding the certainty of hell than John Wesley who wrote,

> If there be no unquenchable fire, no everlasting burnings, there is no dependence upon Scripture. No Hell, no Heaven, no revelation!—STEPHEN HOBHOUSE, *Selected Mystical Writings,* p. 351

Having observed that the traditional stance which has been most prominent in the growing church was to affirm belief in hell, it is now our intent to show how the concept was incorporated in the three prevailing variations. The presuppositions are all of ancient origin and may be briefly described as follows.

1. *Everlasting Punishment.* The theory has been defended by such church fathers as Tertullian of the second century, father of Latin theology; Augustine of the fourth century, spiritual leader for both Roman Catholic and Protestant churches; Thomas Aquinas who lived in the thirteenth century and became the authoritarian of Catholicism; the sixteenth century Father of the Protestant Reformation, Martin Luther; the creator of Calvinism who lived contemporary with Luther, John Calvin; and the Wesley brothers who brought Methodism into existence in the dark days of the eighteenth century in England.

Preachers of repute who have proclaimed the doctrine are John Chrysostom and Ambrose (fourth century), John Wyclif (fourteenth century), Jerome Savonarola (fifteenth century), George Whitefield and Jonathan Edwards (eighteenth century), Charles Spurgeon and D. L. Moody of the nineteenth century, Billy Sunday at the turn of the present century, and Billy Graham whose voice is still being heard around the world.

Creeds and classics which espouse the belief include the Athanasian Creed, the Augsburg Confession, Augustine's *The City of God,* Lombard's *Summa Theologica,* Calvin's *Institutes of the Christian Religion,* Dante's *Inferno,* Milton's *Paradise Lost,* and Bunyan's *Pilgrim's Progress.*

2. *Annihilation or Conditional Immortality.* This concept argues that evil is not eternal. God and good will last forever, but Satan and evil will be completely destroyed. Persons who have held this theory and whose teachings have left their influence upon the modern world include Thomas Hobbes (seventeenth century); John Locke who died shortly after the beginning of the eighteenth century; Richard Whatley, Richard Rothe, Albert Ritschl, Horace Bushnell, Franz Delitzsch, Henry Drummond, and Robert Dale of the nineteenth century; and Alfred Garvie who died in 1945.

3. *Universalism.* This idea first propounded by Origen of the third century insists that God will never cease to seek His erring children, that punishment is not retributive but remedial and corrective. Among well-known persons convinced by this theory are Charles Chauncy and Immanuel Kant (eighteenth century), Friedrich Schleiermacher and Johann Neander who overlapped both the eighteenth and nineteenth centuries, Alfred Tennyson of the nineteenth, and Leslie Weatherhead of London Methodism.

In the next three chapters we will take a look at each of these specified views of hell. In no case will our study be exhaustive. The field is far too broad for a treatment of the nature of this book which sets as its goal a presentation which can easily be read at one setting by the concerned layman.

Discussion Questions for Chapter 2

1. *Why has modern demythologizing of the Bible failed to rid man's subconscious of the thought of hell?*
2. *In what way is a denial of hell realistic? scientific? escapism?*
3. *What does modern man mean by the transference of hell from the hereafter to the here and now? How has this altered the Biblical concept?*
4. *Explain how early excesses and abuses in preaching have contributed to the decline in contemporary discussions of hell.*

5. *Show in what way hell may be thought of as the fulfillment of one's desire. In what manner it insures the mercy of God upon him who is eternally incarcerated there.*
6. *In the light of the Biblical view of hell and heaven as opposites, what must hell be like?*
7. *Name the three prevailing variations on the concept of hell and recall two supporters for each one.*

3

Eternal Punishment?

Of all the more traditional concepts relating to the doctrine of hell, everlasting punishment of the wicked has always been the orthodox theory. Most likely it always will be. It is true that the fathers of the church held differing views of the way in which punishment after death would be meted out, but the predominant belief was that of eternal punishment. Gibbon insists that one of the major causes of the growth of the Ancient Church was its belief in endless torment for those outside the fellowship (*The Decline and Fall of the Roman Empire,* II, p. 142).

Medieval churchmen were in complete agreement with the severity of the doctrine as understood by the earlier church and the later reformers saw no reason to adjust it. Actually, both Protestants and Roman Catholics continued the emphasis until the eighteenth century rebellion which was brought about, in part at least, by the excessive and stringent manner in which hell was proclaimed. By the nineteenth century the rebellion had mushroomed into a monstrous antiforce which has intimidated those few Christians who still believe in the doctrine in today's world. It is significant that only in the last two hundred years has there been any marked resistance to the idea.

Undoubtedly, the extreme forms of presentation to which we have referred would include the unfeeling and careless way in which even young children were consigned by Calvin and others to a fiery hell. Horace Bushnell, having lost one of his children at an early age, was reacting against the heartless manner in which "infants a span long" were preached into *gehenna*. This unfortunate emphasis proclaimed by some of the reformers and their theological offspring has left either an attitude of total rejection or a sense of embarrassed regret in the minds of later generations. Aware of the importance of subjecting children to the truth from the very beginning, there is not only a right and wrong way of doing it, but the age and understanding of the young must be considered as well. Great care must be taken lest we force more upon children than they are able to receive. It is true that multitudes have objected to the theory of everlasting punishment *per se*. But it is also true that greater multitudes have reacted to the calloused manner in which the doctrine has been proclaimed.

A classic story has made the circuit among the more evangelically oriented churches about a congregation which was looking for a new pastor. Strange as it may seem, the guest preachers on the two consecutive weekends chose the same text and preached on hell. Both were Biblical in their content and gave evidence of homiletical skill and careful preparation. Neither was deficient in the art of public speaking. When the pulpit committee met to make a decision there was no question about whom to choose. The vote to call the second man was unanimous. When some of the parishioners inquired as to how the selection was made the committee chairman explained that both men had done a satisfactory job. The subtle difference lay in their attitudes. Both had warned the people that they were going to hell unless they repented of their sins. The first, however, seemed to be glad of it while the other's heart was obviously broken over the plight of his listeners.

There are inevitably some who will object to the theory of everlasting punishment as being insensitive to human feelings regardless as to how it is dressed. Theologians and preachers have always been keenly aware that there is only so much which can be done to make the idea of hell attractive. As a result, many seminary and parish leaders have refused to mention the subject as though it were bad taste to bring it up. Whatever accusations may be directed toward ministers for insisting on the validity of the doctrine, the faithful minister cannot afford to be irresponsible with the Scripture but must follow where it leads.

Philo, the Jewish apologist whose writings present a comprehensive explanation of the intellectual and theological life of diaspora Jewry in Hellenistic Egypt, clearly states that the fate of the wicked Jews in *tartarus* (see the earlier clarification of this word in the introductory section) will be eternal. Whatever may be the exact meaning of this word it is clear that this Jewish apologist was referring to that place which Christians call hell. It is important to note that Philo lived at the beginning of the Christian Era and enunciates the generally-held view of both the orthodox Jews and the Judeo-Christian community of that period. Hell was accepted as being, for all practical purposes, endless. The city dump had been burning and maggot-infested for as long as the disciples could remember and there was no reason to assume that it would ever end. It even seemed fitting that, as refuse was cast away and burned rather than allowed to contaminate the whole community, men and women ought not be permitted to befoul the atmosphere of the life to come but should be cast into a place of separation and destruction when their useless lives justified such an end.

Isaac Watts was certain that everlasting hell was the unadulterated view presented in the New Testament. In his own straightforward way, he states:

> If Christ and His apostles, who were taught by Him and by His blessed Spirit, assert this punishment shall be eternal, who shall dare to contradict them? Who is there so rash and confident as to say, "This torment shall not be everlasting, this worm one day shall die, and this fire shall be quenched?" Does it not approach to the crime of contradicting the Almighty and the true God?—*The World to Come,* pp. 394, 395

Wesley also had no doubt about the duration of hell. In writing to a young soldier about his relationship with Christ, the Oxford scholar declares, "Whoever is once cast into that lake of fire shall be tormented day and night for ever and ever. O eternity! eternity! Who can tell the length of eternity?" (*The Works of the Rev. John Wesley, A.M.*, XI, 199.) Of that misery St. Francis reasons that if a little insect in one's ear makes one night seem so long, the endless night of eternity will be terrible to contemplate. And Dante affirms that the inscription above the portals which open into hell reads:

WHEN YE STEP ACROSS THE SILL OF HELL
ABANDON YE ALL HOPE!

The most apocalyptic writing in the New Testament is the Book of Revelation. While it has already been agreed that the word *gehenna* is not employed by the author, it is also unanimously affirmed that "the lake of fire" is an expression to be equated in meaning with hell as used in the Synoptic Gospels. When the revelator describes the end of the age, he pictures the devil as being thrown "into the lake of fire and brimstone where the beast and the false prophet were, and they will be tormented day and night forever and ever" (Revelation 20:10 RSV). Later in the same chapter he continues, ". . . if anyone's name was not found written in the book of life, he was thrown into the lake of fire" (v. 15). It is consistently argued throughout the Book of Revelation that hell is everlasting.

One favorite passage which has been used more than any other by the advocates of everlasting punishment for the wicked is Matthew 25 where the judgment scene is graphically depicted. C. H. Dodd speaks for those who doubt the authenticity of the passage. With a terse statement he clears the New Testament of the Parable of the Sheep and the Goats (which he calls "a short apocalypse") by saying, "It does not conform to the parabolic type, but belongs to the same class as the judgment scenes in Enoch and other apocalypses" (*The Parables of the Kingdom*, p. 63). He assumes that the judgment scene was composed to give dramatic force to Matthew 25:40, 45 and its parallels Matthew 10:40–42 and Mark 9:37.

On the other side of the argument is A. M. Hunter who just as convincingly writes:

> This passage is one of the supreme glories of the New Testament, and, despite signs of stylization by the evangelist, contains too many originalities not to go back to Jesus Himself. . . . Our verdict must therefore be that, despite evidences of Matthean stylization, the parable is substantially genuine.—*Interpreting the Parables,* pp. 89, 90, 118

It is true that the word *gehenna* is not found in Matthew 25, but equivalent to this concept is the idea employed in the story. The matter of *everlasting* punishment is contingent on the meaning of the Greek word *aionios* rendered *eternal.* R. A. Torrey pursued what seems to have been a clear logic when he wrote over half a century ago:

> It is said by those who would have us believe that there is hope even in hell, that the word Aionios, translated "everlasting," does not necessarily mean never-ending. . . . What it does mean, therefore, in any given instance, must be determined by the context. In Matthew 25:46, we read, "These shall go away into everlasting punishment: but the righteous into life eternal." The word which is translated "everlasting" in the first part of the verse is the same as the word translated "eternal" in the latter part of the passage, and what it means in the last half of the verse, it must also mean in the first part of the verse. But no one doubts that in the last part of the verse it means absolutely endless; therefore, it must mean that in the first part of the verse.—*The Higher Criticism and the New Theology,* pp. 267, 268

A modern writer follows the same logic in explaining the use of the debated Greek term:

> The strongest evidence that the word "aionios" is meant to teach the endlessness of the punishment of the wicked is the fact that the same word is used to describe the blessed life of the godly. In a number of passages the two uses of

the word lie side by side. Only a violent twisting of meaning can lead to any other conclusion than this: if "aionios"
describes life which is endless, so must "aionios" describe
endless punishment. Here the doctrine of heaven and the
doctrine of hell stand or fall together.—HARRY BUIS, *The
Doctrine of Eternal Punishment*, p. 49

Speaking of this parable in Matthew 25 as it relates to hell, a
church leader of an earlier decade concludes without reservation
that "the doom of the rejected is explicitly stated to be 'eternal
punishment.' Baron von Hugel is perfectly right in saying that if
we follow the New Testament 'the essence of hell lies assuredly,
above all, in its unendingness" (W. R. Inge, *What Is Hell?*, pp.
6, 7).

The Congregational minister, theologian, philosopher, and
president of Princeton University in the eighteenth century is the
most noteworthy example of the use of hell in the evangelism
which characterized the first eighteen hundred years of Christianity. Though Jonathan Edwards preached far more than hellfire-and-brimstone, he is remembered for his strong emphasis on
the fear of hell in bringing men to Christ. In his classic sermon,
"Sinners in the Hands of an Angry God," which left people
prostrate in the aisle before the angry Judge, he picturesquely
portrays the fate of sinful man.

> The God that holds you over the pit of hell, much as one
> holds a spider, or some loathsome insect over the fire, abhors
> you, and is dreadfully provoked: His wrath towards you
> burns like fire; He looks upon you as worthy of nothing else,
> but to be cast into the fire; He is of purer eyes than to bear
> to have you in His sight; you are ten thousand times more
> abominable in His eyes than the most hateful venomous
> serpent is in ours.

In another address, "The Christian Pilgrim," Edwards lashes out
again:

> The bulk of mankind are hasting onward in the broad
> way to destruction; which is, as it were, filled up with the

multitude that are going in it with one accord. And they are every day going into hell out of this broad way by thousands. Multitudes are continually flowing down into the great lake of fire and brimstone, as some mighty river constantly disembogues its water into the ocean.

It has been argued often by advocates of the doctrine of everlasting punishment for the wicked that the idea is necessary to a consistent view of the basic presuppositions on which the redemptive mission of Christ does rest. The rejection of endless punishment as the end of the wicked is usually related to the denial of other doctrines which seem to be a part of the Biblical package which includes original sin, substitutionary atonement, and blood redemption. The coming of Jesus into the world and the death of Christ on the cross demands a recognition of man's terrible plight, his tragic fate. Unless man was in desperate trouble which was of eternal consequences the coming of Christ and His crucifixion were of little significance. *The keystone of our faith is the doctrine of hell, because without this truth there is no justifiable reason for the necessity of the cross and the urgency of the preaching of the gospel to the whole world.* Unless there is a hell—and it is eternal—adherents of the doctrine presume that the danger in which man existed was not grave enough to demand the sacrifice of God's own Son. The atonement means absolutely nothing without the fact of hell.

Other than their dogmatic affirmation that the New Testament teaches eternal punishment, advocates of this doctrine argue from two points of view based on what appears to be sound logic. First, if there is an everlasting heaven for the saints there must also be an everlasting hell for the wicked. Second, unless hell is eternal punishment of the most severe kind the death of Christ on the cross was a solution for sin which was far too drastic. No one can begin to explain all the mysteries involved in the concept of hell. We are conscious of this human limitation when confronted with the stark reality of so sobering a doctrine. In recognition of this fact we can make a summary statement in the conclusion of this section.

There is little question that the proponents of a kind of hell which embraces the terrors of punishment that is everlasting are Biblical. Some will contend that the Bible also suggests other possible interpretations of the concept of *gehenna*. Whatever the reader may think about such a contention, he will be forced to admit that the doctrine of everlasting punishment is indeed Biblical. It is literally impossible to detour around that fact. In addition to this basic truth is the impressive gallery of dedicated and capable Christian scholars who have defended the position. And what is possibly as intriguing as anything else is the caliber of men and women within the Christian community in this day who hold to the doctrine without apology.

Discussion Questions for Chapter 3

1. *What does John mean by the expression "lake of fire"?*
2. *Discuss the parable of the sheep and the goats (Matthew 25) and show why it confirms belief in* everlasting *punishment.*
3. *In what way can it be said that the essence of hell is its "unendingness"?*
4. *Why does a rejection of the doctrine of everlasting hell reflect on one's attitude toward other major doctrines of the Bible?*
5. *Explain how the cross of redemption was a necessity because of the horror of endless hell.*
6. *If hell is not endless, can we be sure of heaven? Explain.*
7. *Considering the strong Biblical support for this concept, why do so few Christian scholars hold unapologetically to the doctrine?*

4

Conditional Immortality?

The annihilation of the wicked, or conditional immortality, has never been a widely-held theory. This is partly due to the fact that most people who give any serious thought to hell either accept the traditional and orthodox doctrine of everlasting punishment or reject the whole idea and believe that no one will be lost. As regards hell, it is almost always an either/or position which leaves no room for a kind of eternal discontinuance.

To suggest that anything can ever be completely destroyed does not ring true at all. The suggestion that there is something which can finally cease to be is even contrary to the axiom (though some are now challenging this old scientific rule of thumb) that nothing is either created or destroyed. It is true that the scientific law has always related to matter, but when matter is transformed into energy rather than destroyed by burning, one quickly senses how difficult is the task of distinguishing between material and metaphysical.

To believe that man and his consciousness can cease to be is to annul the concept which holds human life to be endowed with eternal dimensions. And this is precisely what the annihilationist believes. The theory rests on the presupposition that man is not immortal by birth as the Platonists taught. The distinction between the annihilationist and the Platonist is simply that the latter believed in the immortality of the soul in contradistinction to the body while the annihilationist contends that man is a

creature with no natural immortality at all. Man, on the basis of
the annihilationist's theory, becomes eternal only as he responds
to God who brings him to life. There is no everlasting death as
there can be everlasting life. Men who do not find life in God
which surpasses human creatureliness simply cease to exist at
death. That is, death is the end for the unregenerate. There is
nothing beyond that point in time.

Tillich believes that everlasting existence belongs to the
redeemed and that extinction is the reward of the unredeemed.
He clarifies this point for us:

> Eternity as a quality of the divine life cannot be attri-
> buted to a being which as condemned is separated from the
> divine life. Where the divine love ends, being ends; con-
> demnation can only mean that the creature is left to the
> non-being it has chosen. The symbol "eternal death" is more
> expressive when interpreted as self-exclusion from eternal
> life and consequently from being.—*Systematic Theology*,
> II, p. 284

While there have always been individuals and small groups
who held to the doctrine of annihilation of the wicked and
repudiated everlasting punishment, the most prominent groups
in recent years are the Adventists and Jehovah's Witnesses.
Allowances must be made for variations on the general theme,
but the basic idea is held by both groups. The idea emerged as
early as the second century of the Christian era. Justin Martyr
believed that "souls both die and are punished" (*Dialogue with
Trypho*, 5). Tatian said of the unregenerate soul that "it tends
downwards towards matter and dies with the flesh" (*An Address
to the Greeks*, 13). Irenaeus suggests that the man who refuses
God destroys his chance of everlasting continuance (*Against the
Heresies*, 2, 34, 3, 4).

To assume that punishment will endure for a period, depend-
ing on the degree of the evil done by the wicked, and then cease
is in keeping with one school of annihilationists. The only difference between this view and that of the advocates of purgatory
is that, in the latter case, the evil is purged and the wicked

released while, in the former instance, the sinner dies with the punishment of evil. If the created order is to become fully God's in the age to come, then evil and its penalty must cease to be a part of that new world. Every enemy of God and righteousness must be totally and finally destroyed if God is to be ultimately victorious. Evil cannot be allowed to continue to exist even in the state of punishment. Its very existence negates the full and complete victory of God over all that has opposed Him. Often a distinction is made between the consequences of sin—which are endless—and the suffering which is said to terminate at some point beyond death.

Annihilationists are also found who emphasize the point that extinction is the result of the disintegrating effect of sin gradually worked out in the life of the evil doer. Man, by his wickedness, eventually destroys himself until there is nothing left to live. Oliver C. Quick speaks to this argument as well as to the theory that the wicked may suffer for a while before final cessation.

We conclude . . . that the ultimate issue of the rejection of God's love must be God's final abandonment of the soul to the consequences of its own corruption. In the Gospel of St. Matthew God's final doom on his unrepentant people is pronounced in the words, "Your house is left unto you" . . . And the prayer of Charles Wesley's hymn, "leave, ah, leave me not alone," is not to be distinguished in meaning from the pattern of the Litany, "From everlasting damnation, good Lord, deliver us." The soul which suffers that doom will inevitably perish in the final passing away of the sin-tainted world with which it has chosen to identify itself.
                                        —*Doctrines of the Creed,* pp. 257, 258

It is possible, according to the conditionalists (annihilationists), not alone to lose the capacity to respond to God by sinfulness and be forced to suffer for it, but to fully cease to be at all. Final dissolution is a solemn and haunting thing to think about but it may be much easier to accept by those who are repelled at the thought of being forced to exist endlessly in torment. Hell, according to this interpretation, has nothing to do with duration in time. It has only to do with quality, a completeness of rejection which implies an "end" rather than a lack of it. Anything less than such a termination would by that very fact be less than final. Strange as it may appear, some argue for the same result from the opposite stance. These proponents of conditional immortality contend that hell does have to do with a duration in time but that such duration infers a "fullness of time" rather than timelessness. The conditionalist seems to have a built-in weakness in that if hell is termination it is also irremediable and if irremediable it is also endless because naturally changeless.

Advocates of this position often claim that a continuance of punishment forever would be needless. When the earth is finally cleansed of evil, the most rational assumption would be that evil should die, that no vestige of it should remain alive or sensitive in the New Age. This is what D. P. Walker has in mind when he reasons:

> Hell's greatest strength, its deterrent effect in this life, also has its weak points, and is moreover closely linked to a grave weakness: the uselessness of hell after the end of the world.—*The Decline of Hell,* p. 40

One must not rule out the possibility that the doctrine of conditional immortality could be a form of wish-fulfillment. While one may not be able, in good conscience, to rule out a future world of existence or retributive punishment on sin, the severity of hell can be mitigated by arguing for its impermanence. Aldous Huxley, far from a believer himself, sensed this possibility when he put words into the mouth of Bruno.

> Bruno has suggested that no sorrow should be felt for those prepared for death and Eustace, the man of the world, says, "No nonsense about immortality! None of your wishful thinking!" But Bruno softly answers, "Yet, annihilation would be pretty convenient, wouldn't it? What about the wish to believe that?"—*Time Must Have a Stop,* p. 107

It may be that man is vividly portrayed in a character like Herman Melville, the novelist, who, while having great love for

Christ, was never quite sure of his own beliefs. He was really skeptical of existence of any kind after death. Nathaniel Hawthorne was chatting with him in Liverpool in 1856 when Melville began talking about the uncertainty of life beyond death and affirmed that he had about made up his mind to be annihilated. Hawthorne was impressed by the fact, however, that the prospects of such seemed to bring no rest to Melville. Indeed, no one of us can find rest until we become convinced of some belief.

Nicolas Berdyaev, the Russian existentialist, who repudiates eternal punishment as "morally revolting" and reincarnation as "the nightmare of endless incarnations," is more deeply convinced than most about the *end* of hell. Hell "belongs to time and therefore is temporal. . . . Hell is an aeon or an aeon of aeons, as it says in the Gospel, but not eternity. Only those are in hell who have not entered eternity but have remained in time" (*The Destiny of Man,* p. 279). Such theological jargon is often hard to grasp by the uninitiated layman but it appears that either hell is confined to this life or to a span of "time" after death prior to the commencement of eternity.

It is always difficult for Christian thinkers to fully reconcile the love of God and everlasting punishment. Thus, varied theories have been advanced suggesting ways to either explain or annul the concept of eternal torment. In view of the strong statements of the New Testament which warn of everlasting hell, the subject is usually approached with caution and great reservation. Men of God who love men and also respect the Scriptures are often torn between the doctrine of everlasting punishment on the one hand and an annulment of hell on the other. Annihilationists appear to be in a kind of struggle to hold to both the severity of hell and the humaneness of Christianity without actually embracing either. It is a gray mid-world between two poles of doctrinal thought. As such, most of us find the concept of conditional immortality suspect.

Discussion Questions for Chapter 4

1. *Why might we refer to conditional immortality as an "in-between theory"?*

2. *Show how the whole concept of natural immortality is under-cut by this extinction theory.*
3. *How can annihilation of the wicked be said to be required for total divine victory?*
4. *What is meant by personal disintegration or dissolution?*
5. *Why do some insist that hell would be useless after the end of the world?*
6. *Could the doctrine of conditional immortality be a form of wish-fulfillment? Explain your answer.*
7. *Is the idea of annihilation an attempt to be scriptural without negating humaneness?*

5

Universalism— Will All Be Saved?

The basic doctrine of universalism is that all men will finally be saved—that ultimately none will be lost. Advocates of the theory believe that punishment is remedial, that God's nature is love, and that the mercy of the Lord cannot be satisfied with either partial salvation (annihilation) or everlasting punishment. The first great preacher of this doctrine was Origen who believed that fire is purifying and quoted Malachi the prophet to prove his point to the pagan Celsus. The passage reads, "But who can endure the day of his coming, and who can stand when he appears? For he is like a refiner's fire and like fullers' soap; he will sit as a refiner and purifier of silver, and he will purify the sons of Levi and refine them like gold and silver, till they present right offerings to the Lord" (Malachi 3:2, 3 RSV). He even had hope for the rebel angels and, unbelievable as it seems, could imagine a day when even Satan would be redeemed!

Another early defender of the doctrine was Gregory of Nyssa who believed that punishment is always remedial and illustrated it by comparing hell to a surgeon's knife which, though painful, is corrective (*The Great Catechism*, 26). Though the idea was considered heretical, it was revived by Scotus Erigena in the ninth century only to be short-lived. Not again did anyone dare to resurrect the concept, except in suggestions of Gregory of Nyssa, Gregory Nazianzen (*Orations*, X, 36), and Jerome (*Commentary on Ephesians*, III, 10) until the seventeenth century. In the

eighteenth century William Law was influenced by universalism
(*Selected Mystical Writings of William Law,* p. 196) as was
Tennyson (see his poem "In Memoriam") and Friedrich Schleiermacher (*The Christian Faith*) in the nineteenth. Karl Barth's
view is that all men are elected and redeemed in Jesus Christ
and need only to know this first-hand (*Church Dogmatics,* IV, 1,
129). Emil Brunner rejects the Barthian brand of universalism
but argues for a second chance by which those who do not accept
Christ here will be given an opportunity in the world to come
(*Eternal Hope*). Paul Tillich suggests that Christianity has made
three important attempts to lessen the theory that the moment of
death is decisive for a man's final destiny. They are listed in the
following order: reincarnation, intermediate state (bodiless animation), and purgatory (*Systematic Theology,* III, 416).

While some have cast aside the Biblical record as having no
authority in areas where human reason objects, most universalists
have great respect for the Scripture. Occasionally some flippant
soul will demand that the Bible is "out of it" and need not restrict
us any longer, that creeds formulated by the Ancient Church are
of no particular significance today, but such persons can be found
in many schools of religious thought.

Most sensitive Christian scholars have far greater respect for
the sacred writings of the Christian church and seek honestly to
interpret them. In practically every case, a thoroughgoing universalism is built on a conviction that the theory is upheld by
the Bible. Often, Paul's sweeping references to the salvation of
"all" men (Romans 5:18; 11:25, 26; 1 Corinthians 15:22; 2 Corinthians 5:14) are used to support the universalist's theory. These
passages must not be seen in the role of supportive Scripture for
universalism. While the Apostle Paul is affirming the universality
of the gospel, it is obvious that he is insisting that all will believe
at the end, but this is far from the view which insists that *every*
individual will be *saved.* Some will believe without repentance
and some will be certain to believe when it is too late at the
judgment to come. The passages to which we have referred in
the writings of Paul must be read in the context of his other
words of condemnation (Romans 2:5–10) if a full view is to be

presented. Unless the overall context of the New Testament is invoked one can prove almost anything from holy Scripture.

Often churchmen have hinted at universalism while at the same time obviously fearful of positive statements. In his ponderous work on the life of Christ, Alfred Edersheim muses thoughtfully:

> . . . it seems at least an exaggeration to put the alternatives thus: absolute eternity of punishment—and, with it, of the state of rebellion which it implies, since it is unthinkable that rebellion should absolutely cease, and yet punishment continue; annihilation; or else universal restoration. Something else is at least thinkable, that may not lie within these hard and fast lines of demarcation. It is at least conceivable that there may be . . . an unfolding of the germ of grace, present before death, invisible though it may have been to other men, and that in the end of what we call time or "dispensation," only that which is morally incapable of transformation—be it man or devils—shall be cast into the lake of fire and brimstone.—*The Life and Times of Jesus the Messiah,* II, p. 795

We cannot easily classify Edersheim as a universalist because he leaves the door open for "something" to be cast into the fire. His logic would lead him to consider seriously the basic premise on which universalism is constructed—that God will not fail in the Messianic mission to redeem the world.

Near the turn of the century, J. Paterson-Smyth concluded that we are "free to believe that the Judge of all the earth will do right—that Hell as well as Heaven is within the confines of His dominion—that evil shall not last forever; that . . . the trend of Scripture moves towards the golden age, the final victory of good" (*The Gospel of the Hereafter,* pp. 195, 196). There can be no argument that the Judge "will do right." What man must acknowledge is that He does not have to do what we human beings have decided to be *right*. Divine justice is so far beyond the poor earthly copy that the prophet can rightly affirm for the Lord, "For my thoughts are not your thoughts, neither are your ways my ways" (Isaiah 55:8 RSV). We have no right to suppose that our judgments are right. Rather we must admit that whatever God may do in the world to come *will be right!*

The suggestion is sometimes made, in keeping with this dangerous brand of inductive reasoning, that the Psalmist exclaims, ". . . if I make my bed in hell, behold thou art there" (Psalms 139:8). What could God be doing there if not to rescue and save? Could He be there to torment? These are haunting questions, but it must be noted that the word used in the original Hebrew is *sheol* and denotes the abode of the dead. This is not the final place of punishment denoted by the Greek *gehenna* but rather the equivalent of *hades*. And the context clearly has to do with the fact that it is impossible to go anywhere in the universe where God is not to be found. It has nothing to do with the concept of either salvation or punishment. The context is always the key.

William Barclay struggles with the problem of ultimate failure in the divine plan of redemption when examining the creedal statements. We can understand his dilemma when seen from a purely human perspective.

> It seems to us that if God is the God who is the God and Father of our Lord Jesus Christ, and if the total impression of the Gospel is true, we may dare to hope that when time ends God's family will be complete, for surely we must think in terms, not of a king who is satisfied with a victory which destroys his enemies, but of a Father who can never be content when even a single child of his is outside the circle of his love.—*The Apostle's Creed for Everyman*, p. 239

If it is possible to overdo the Christian doctrine of divine love, it is surely at this point. Love not only "covers a multitude of sins" (1 Peter 4:8 RSV) but it is allowed to blot out "the total impression of the Gospel." Perhaps it needs to be remembered that eternal destruction is not God's doing but man's, the Father may never be "content" with His creation, and eternal separation from God after death does not cancel His love (Luke 16:25). Even in *hades,* the prelude to *gehenna* in the case of the rich man (here the context must be considered as always), the man in torment was addressed most affectionately!

Also enamored with what may well be a one-sided view of the love of God, Leslie Weatherhead reasons that "the Good Shepherd at last will bring every soul into the fold, for he himself gave men the picture of the Good Shepherd not content with 99 percent of successes, but seeking the lost sheep 'until he find it'" (*The Christian Agnostic,* pp. 285, 286). What may be overlooked here is that not all people are among the *sheep.* Jesus was referring to those who are already a part of the legitimate sheepfold of God (John 10). The sheep which had strayed was one of the shepherd's own which bore the brand of its master. In the judgment scene in Matthew 25, we see more clearly that all the sheep are saved but there are some *goats* which are not so fortunate. God will be "successful" with the sheep (those who are honestly a part of His sheepfold) but those among the goats (the multitude which never enters in at all) who are lost will not render the victory of the Lord any less. At this point, as in others mentioned previously, Scripture must be interpreted in light of the entire New Testament, not just the part which confirms our predetermined suppositions.

Having looked briefly at the argument for universalism from the logic of divine success, we turn now to investigate the two most widely-held theories about how ultimate and universal salvation may come to pass.

More and more we are hearing advanced in Christian circles the idea of remedial suffering as descriptive of hell. A modern writer observes this direction which theology is taking when he states, "Hell itself is transformed from the ultimate state of the lost into a means of grace—a neo-Protestant purgatory of sorts" (Carl Henry, *Evangelicals at the Brink of Crisis,* p. 27). Obviously, the idea is not at all new. As long as man has had a defective understanding of the horrendous nature of sin he has refused to admit that the consequences of a life of sinfulness could be as severe as some have believed. Though we have not used the Roman Catholic place name of purgatory, the non-Biblical idea has wide acceptance among the descendants of Martin Luther.

It is not at all unusual to hear churchmen excusing their moral shortcomings lightly as though their natures can be corrected in some other world where it will be simpler than here.

When we insist that repentance and redemption are still open to man after death, we are running directly counter to the teaching of the Bible. If we are willing to discard the authority of the Scriptures we may well hold to any view which sounds reasonable to us. The story of Lazarus and the rich man referred to above is crystal clear in its rejection of another chance for men who have heard the story prior to their deaths. The only New Testament word about purging fires has to do with the burning fire of the Holy Spirit who can burn out the evil of man's life "with unquenchable fire" (Matthew 3:12, cf. Acts 2). Every man should run to the fire, but the fire is in this life and not in the next. If there should be fire in the world to come it will undoubtedly be the kind from which every man would recoil!

Human rationalization inevitably leads us astray. Our only touchstone of eternal reality is found in the Scripture. Austin Farrer contends, "It seems strange indeed that so practical and pressing a truth as that of purgatory should be dismissed, while so remote and impractical a doctrine as the absolute everlasting-ness of hell should be insisted on" (*Saving Belief*, p. 154). Yet, the "impractical" is the basic teaching of the entire Bible while the "practical" has its origin in man's search for truth outside the written Word of God. If one is to build his system of belief on what is "practical and pressing" there is no way of knowing what kind of humanistic God he will worship or what sort of religious institution he will build.

When Protestants substitute a fuzzy doctrine of purgatory for the clear Biblical concept of hell we claim for our brainchild even more than our Roman Catholic brethren. The Roman theory never included within it the idea that all men would finally be saved. The disciplinary and curative punishment was not for everyone. In Catholicism there is no substitution of purgatory for hell. Both doctrines are embraced. In Protestantism, however, where a belief in the former is found all traces of an acceptance of the latter are dismissed.

Not many are willing to say emphatically whether there is to be an opportunity for altering one's destiny after death. This is manifestly due to the fact that there is no clear warrant in the Bible for such a conjecture. Ralph Sockman assumes that "where there is life there is possibility of growth" (*How to Believe,* p. 222), while Buttrick more cautiously reasons, "As to the possibilities of moral change hereafter, who can speak?" (*Parables of Jesus,* p. 69.) A lack of dogmatism is commendable in areas of belief where there is no scriptural clarity, but why we would lack certainty in this area is difficult to understand.

Related to the whole concept of universalism is the old philosophy of transcendentalism made popular by Emerson. This idea held that every soul is a part of the "oversoul" of the universe. To use a common metaphor, man is a spark of the universal Flame and will eventually return to it to be absorbed into the One Soul of all time. Occasionally, in the twentieth century, someone seems to border on the old Emersonian theory without calling it such. And since it does relate to universalism in its insistence that all souls will become once more a part of what they were, it is worth noting at this point. Hell, according to this nebulous theory, is a training school for fragments of the Eternal Self which must be disciplined into final merger. The soul of man is only a spark of the divine Flame and will finally be reabsorbed into It.

No one has summed up the theory of universalism as it is related to remedial suffering and transcendentalism any better than Stephen Hobhouse.

It would take too long here to argue fully the case for universalism, the belief, which seems to me to approach certainty, that all created spirits, whether human or angelic, however degraded by self-centered pride (the root of all sin), by cruelty, or by sensuality, will eventually, though perhaps after long periods of purgation, that is of purifying disciplinary suffering, be restored by way of penitence and full forgiveness to the harmony and beauty of their original existence in God.—*A Discourse on the Life to Come,* p. 69

Reincarnation is the oldest known doctrine of life after death. It is still devoutly believed by the Hindu and is becoming increasingly reputable in the western world. Multitudes of Christians have become enamored with the idea, and contend that hell may be finally escaped by repeated performances of human existence, each one an improvement over the preceding one. Having experimented with an abundance of psychic phenomena, Weatherhead reflects on the whole matter of the human spirit.

> One wonders why men have so readily accepted the idea of life *after* death and so largely, in the West, discarded the idea of a life *before* birth. So many arguments for a one-way immortality seems to me *cogent* for a two-way life outside the present body.—*The Christian Agnostic,* p. 303

Here again, the argument is formed by an accumulation of human building blocks created without due respect for the written Word. According to the Bible, only Christ can be said to have existed before His birth in Bethlehem.

The theory of life before birth for man comes from the ancients by way of Greek philosophy. It does not come from either the Jewish or the Christian Scriptures. One can easily see how a theory can be influenced by Christian theology, Hindu reincarnation, and Buddhist transmigration and be a syncretistic mixture of all three. Thus it often becomes difficult to detect whether the thinker is a Hindu or a Buddhist with Christian sympathies or a Christian with leanings toward aspects of Hinduism or Buddhism.

The Christian should have a clearer understanding of what he believes than this. When he does not, it is inevitably because he does not have a thorough grounding in the Word itself. We get ourselves into trouble by being more familiar with philosophy and science than with the Scriptures. What man says is never a substitute for what God says. If the Bible is spurned we will go in as many directions as there are ideas in our search for truth. Only if the Word of God is respected and revered will a man be able to give a reason for "the hope that is in [him]" (1 Peter 3:15).

Discussion Questions for Chapter 5

1. *Some argue that endless hell defeats the final plan of God. What do they mean by this and how can the argument be refuted?*
2. *What is the difference between the concept of purgatory and the doctrine of universalism? Could hell be a "means of grace"?*
3. *If there is a second chance for redemption after death, what does this do to a serious attitude toward this life?*
4. *Some suggest that hell is a "training school." If this is true, then what is the value of preparing for eternity while in this world?*
5. *In what way is transcendentalism related to universalism?*
6. *How does universalism fit into the Hindu teaching of reincarnation?*
7. *Is there any Biblical support for universalism? If so, where? If not, where does the idea find its source?*

6

The Nature of God

Over a century ago, churchmen were beginning to say, "I can hardly imagine two propositions more discordant one with the other than that Almighty God is love and that He will torment sinners forever" (T. Davis, *Endless Sufferings Not a Doctrine of Scripture*, p. 56). This is the argument made popular and sold to the American public by John Stuart Mill et al. The presupposition is that a *good* man would not punish anyone forever, therefore, how could a good God do such a thing? If the nature of God is love, then it is impossible to think also of His nature as avenging.

Bruce Barton surmised that God is "not a petulant Creator . . . a stern Judge . . . a vain King . . . a rigid Accountant. . . . Not any of these . . . nothing like these; but a great Companion, a wonderful Friend, a kindly-indulgent, joy-loving Father" (*The Man Nobody Knows*, pp. 61, 62). Undoubtedly, this concept is an extreme reaction to another unfortunate extreme in which God was portrayed as a tyrant who let the redeemed share sadistically in the joy of seeing the wicked suffer. We have done well in ridding ourselves of the mental image of a divine Being who wears a scowl upon His face and is set on seeing to it that man gets what he deserves. But in correcting this image we have fallen into the error of thinking of God as a totally submissive, sentimentally sweet grandfather!

Persons rejecting the doctrine of *gehenna* on the basis of divine love usually turn to the Christian concept of God as Father. It is conceived to be unlikely that a loving Father could ever be so vicious as the concept of hell would suggest. Yet it is true that Jesus warned men to "fear him which is able to destroy both soul and body in hell" (Matthew 10:28). Attempts have been made to interpret this passage as a reference to Satan rather than God but such an interpretation is a glaring example of eisegesis (reading into Scripture what is not there). It does not fit the context at all. While the reference is clearly to God we need not see it as a reflection upon His goodness, rather as an emphasis on His power. John Ellicott contends that "we are not told to think of God as in any case willing to destroy, but only as having the power to inflict that destruction where all offers of mercy and all calls to righteousness have been rejected" (*Ellicott's Commentary*, VI, p. 63). In the epistle of James there is a similar reference to destruction where there is undisputable evidence that He to whom the writer refers is God: "There is one lawgiver, who is able to save and to destroy . . ." (James 4:12).

A contemporary newspaper reporter and distinguished journalist, Louis Cassels, suggests that "the idea that God is capable of righteous wrath, that He punishes errant children, is very disturbing to anyone with this image. But it is a part of what Jesus meant when He spoke of God as 'Our Father in Heaven'" (*The Real Jesus*, p. 46). Those of us who seek to refute the theory that Fatherhood implies leniency—and only leniency—usually argue, as does Cassels, that when Jesus called God "Father," He was not suggesting the modern type of father who is often so permissive as to be ineffective. A father in the first century was the head of his house and demanded obedience. Where there was disobedience, the child was dealt with severely.

There is no reason to equate the divine Fatherhood with softness. How like us it is to get a smug, warm feeling when we think about God, the feeling which a child has when he is sure that he can get away with almost anything. Such a child may call his lenient father *loving* but in his heart he knows better.

He is conscious that there is something wrong with a paternal love which is so superficial that it makes no demands and warns of no consequences. It is impossible to respect such a father, much less to love him, when it is apparent that he is either too weak or too unconcerned to discipline or punish. Man not only takes advantage of such a God; he inwardly despises Him. Nothing less than a divine Being who keeps love and judgment —including punishment—in proper balance is deserving of the name *Father*.

Yet there is an abundance of voices crying out against any representation of God which would convey the idea that there are other attributes of the Eternal Spirit which seek to balance a view of fatherly love. The traditional picture of hell as everlasting punishment for sin is "a libel upon a loving God, making the punishment for sin out of all due proportion, and suggesting that in the case of those so consigned to Hell, God is defeated and evil has had the last word" (A. J. Ebbutt, *Who Do You Say That I Am?*, p. 164). Some have attempted to point out that the Eternal Spirit would be eternally torn apart if He is forced to be both just and loving. He could not weep over the lost and rejoice over their defeat at one and the same time. There is no reason to assume, however, that justice implies a kind of sadistic joy on the part of God. Justice is tempered with love but it is not annulled by it. God could never be said to rejoice over man's punishment but neither could He be said to ignore the disobedience of His creation.

A question in the book of Genesis implies its own answer, "Shall not the Judge of all the earth do right?" (Genesis 18:25.) The question is Abraham's and the patriarch cannot bring himself to believe that the Eternal would wipe out the righteous people of Sodom with the wicked inhabitants of the city. The question, in proper context, relates to both God's mercy and His judgment. Indeed, Abraham believes that He *will* do right. The human predicament, as was pointed out earlier, is in knowing whether our understanding of a particular situation is His and therefore correct. Billy Graham observes that there is no inconsistency between judgment and mercy.

The God who would be merciful must move in mercy
according to the standards of justice and righteousness.
Judgment in no way conflicts with mercy; for if mercy is
to be extended, judgment must be a part of the divine
order. To be merciful without being just is a contradiction.
                                          —*World Aflame*, p. 235

Donald Barnhouse shares this traditional concept as embraced
by most evangelical Christians. Like Graham, he sees no reason
for dispensing with justice in order to insure love. Judgment and
hell are even recognized as necessary to real love.

The nature of God is justice to balance His love. The
fact that God's time of patience will end and He will strike
out in justice is the hope of the sin-cursed universe. If God
does not act to destroy, then we face an eternity of sinfulness. But God is holy and just, and therefore He will destroy. For believers He has already moved to destroy their
sin by placing it on Christ and dealing with it for eternity,
but upon those who will not enter into Christ, the flood of
His wrath must fall. Hell is as much a part of the love story
of God as heaven.—*Genesis*, I, pp. 51, 52

To those who object to hell as a final state of punishment for
wickedness done in this life, we need to direct some penetrating
questions. Do we have the right to ask God to clean the slate,
to cancel man's sin and give him a new bill of spiritual health?
Can we expect Him to come to sinful man's aid and cast his sins
away, never to bring them up against him again? Not after death!
But the glory of the gospel is that this is precisely what we can
expect *now*. Already, on Calvary, God has cancelled our sin and
offered us forgiveness. It is the choice of some, regardless as to
what the Father in heaven has done, to reject that forgiveness.
In such cases there is nothing for God to do but leave them to
their wishes, to leave them alone.

For God to leave man alone is not only to conjure up images
of the most terrible aspect of hell, but it is to infer also that hell
is ultimately man's doing, a matter of personal choice. While

Thomas Aquinas argued that the sinner *deserves* the punishment he receives in hell, Dante believed that man *chooses* his destiny. Though both ideas may be correct, the latter is the argument most often used to bring together the nature of divine love and the reality of hell. Radoslav Tsanoff explains Dante's concept: "The *Inferno* is not so much an account of how sin is punished; it is fundamentally a revelation of what sin *is:* essentially and in the full measure of its fruition. . . . Sin *is* death" (*The Problem of Immortality,* p. 54).

We must never think of hell as being created by God out of a desire to see men suffer. In fact, Matthew remembers hearing Jesus' warning of a judgment day when He would have to say to some, "Depart from me, ye cursed, into the everlasting fire, prepared for the devil and his angels" (Matthew 25:41). This clearly indicates that hell was never meant to be the final abode of man. It was originally brought into existence only for the devil and his coworkers. But the creation of such a place was a risk taken by the Creator. The risk further included man's freedom to choose whom he would serve. And he who chooses to serve the devil will inevitably have to dwell with his own master forever. Men damn themselves to suffering in a hell which God never meant for them. It is man's doing more than God's. In a real sense, hell is not related to divine vengeance but to man's will to dwell apart from God. "It is the direct and logical prolongation of man's own will to sin," writes Robert Gleason. "If a man fixes himself in opposition to God, then hell is only the logical working out of this everlasting opposition" (*The World to Come,* p. 116).

This is to say that the justice of God in hell is not to be construed in any sense as being personal revenge. It would be impossible (if there is anything impossible with God) for God to force forgiveness upon anyone who chooses to walk in his own way of rebellion. When man does not wish to receive grace he does not receive it. And it is argued that those who are among the damned have made that choice. To vindicate such people would be totally against their basic desire.

Question ten of the old Heidelberg Catechism (A.D. 1563) asks: "Will God let man get by with such disobedience and defection" as that which characterizes the wicked? And the dogmatic answer is, "Certainly not, for the wrath of God is revealed from heaven, both against our inborn sinfulness and our actual sins, and he will punish them according to his righteous judgment in time and in eternity. . . ." While this sounds divinely vicious, Andre Pery comments,

> The man who brings down the wrath of God upon himself is in truth rejected. He can no longer avail himself of the privilege of his election. He no longer participates in the life which God has given him. He returns to chaos, to an existence "without ground or meaning." He passes into the camp of the enemy, into the domain of darkness and enmity toward God. Such is the downright misery of man cursed by God.—*The Heidelberg Catechism with Commentary*, p. 35

It is rather clear that Pery means to infer, by expressions such as "man who brings down the wrath of God," that hell is finally man's choice.

A contemporary psychologist logically surmises that "man has a right to choose hell rather than heaven, and, indeed, he might feel better there" (R. F. Hobson, *Hell*, Lecture 93, p. 23). Could God be said to love man if, after having chosen to live apart from the Lord here, one should be forced to dwell with the God whom he does not love in eternity? If God loves man, will He not allow him freedom of choice here and hereafter? Would not to do otherwise invade man's world of choice and face him with no alternative but to live in a house with a family where he does not feel at home? If hell has anything to do with God's love, does it not mean simply that divine love must not refuse man his choice? These are questions which must be considered by persons concerned with *gehenna* as it relates to God's nature. May not Harold O. Brown be right when he says, "Hell has been called 'the most enduring monument to the freedom of the human will'?" (*The Protest of a Troubled Protestant*, p. 213.)

Swedenborg speaks of an equilibrium between heaven and hell which is "an equilibrium between the good that is from heaven and the evil that is from hell, thus that it is a spiritual equilibrium, which in its essence is freedom" (*Heaven and Hell*, p. 391). G. W. Barrett and J. V. L. Casserley have stated it in these words:

> Hell is much more a matter of our having to be, perhaps for all eternity, what in fact through our way of life we have become . . . a destiny which is the inevitable consequence of the shape and direction which [man] has given to his own existence.—*Dialogue on Destiny*, p. 77

The heavenly spirit of George Macdonald says to the late C. S. Lewis,

> There are only two kinds of people in the end: those who say to God, "Thy will be done," and those to whom God says, in the end, "*Thy* will be done." All that are in Hell, choose it. Without this self-choice there could be no Hell. No soul that seriously and constantly desires joy will ever miss it.—*The Great Divorce*, p. 69

Others among us who refuse to put the responsibility, for the punishment associated with hell, on God, speak as follows:

> The sinner is in Hell because he has chosen to be there: God Himself cannot save him against his will. The malicious soul actively rejects God, and malice is beyond God's saving grace. To be saved, man must eagerly turn to Christ in prayer and repentance.—RADOSLAV TSANOFF, *The Problem of Immortality*, p. 57

> He [God] has warned us of the results of false pride and greed and hatred. But if we persist he lets us turn half the world into a hell, because he made us responsible moral agents. And God gives us freedom to make an eternal choice, to make the next life a hell.—WILLIAM WARD, *After Death, What?*, p. 65

The most recent and widely-respected voice to add weight to the above quoted theorists is that of the noted evangelist of the last half of the twentieth century, Billy Graham:

> The Bible teaches that God does not take delight in the fact that men on the broad road are lost and bound for hell. It declares that God loves us. He sent His Son to keep us from being lost. He sent the Holy Spirit to prompt us and convict us of our sins so that we would not be lost. If you are lost, and if you go to hell, it will be by your own deliberate choice, because God never meant you to go there. It is your own decision.—*Decision,* September, 1969

We have sought, in this chapter, to deal with the problem most often confronted in the basic concept of hell—the problem of divine love versus divine judgment. In conclusion, it seems to us that the two facets of the nature of God do not come into conflict with one another. On the contrary, they complement each other and spare us the more difficult problem of having a one-sided God. The concept of hell is rendered more valid, not less, due to the loving nature of the Creator-Redeemer who will have nothing less than the best for us and from us.

Discussion Questions for Chapter 6

1. *Do we have to see God as either a petulant tyrant or an over-indulgent grandfather? Is there no option other than these two extremes?*
2. *Both the Old and New Testaments encourage us to fear God. Does this suggest that man should be afraid of his Creator? Show in what way this neglected aspect of obedience should be understood.*
3. *Does divine Fatherhood mean softness? leniency? Is any concept of fatherhood complete without judgment and punishment?*
4. *Explain how justice and love can dwell together without conflict. Point out the manner in which God's love requires divine justice.*

5. *How can hell be said to negate divine love in light of the God-love which is seen on Calvary? If God has opened a way of salvation now, can it be insisted that hell annuls that present offer?*

6. *In what way is it true that God* sends *no one to hell but man* chooses *his destiny?*

7. *Were God to make hell an impossibility what would this do to the free will of man?*

7

Hell—A Motivating Force in Evangelism

There are at least two kinds of motivation in the evangelistic mission of the church—that which motivates the evangelist to proclaim his message and that which impels the hearer to respond. Of the former kind of motivation there are also two types—that which pushes from within the evangelist's soul, simply because he is a Christian and must tell what he has found, and that which pulls from without. Like Jesus, seeing men as sheep without a shepherd constrains the follower of Christ to share both the pasture and the Shepherd. There have been times when it has been suspected that the preaching of hell by the Judeo-Christian prophets has been almost totally subjective in motivation and often selfish.

The impression one gets in reading Irenaeus and Tertullian is that they get real satisfaction out of knowing that the wicked will suffer untold anguish in hell. It must be recalled that these persons lived in days of terrible persecution and such reactions, though not exemplary, were somewhat understandable. For Thomas Aquinas to relish the thought of eternal punishment for the wicked was another matter altogether. The idea of rejoicing at the suffering of another is of pagan origin. Though some have accused Jonathan Edwards of similar motivation, a more thorough reading of his works would indicate that the driving force was rather a deep respect for the sovereignty of God and the desperate plight of the sinner. Edwards insisted in *The Distin-*

guishing Marks that some think it an objectionable thing "to fright persons to heaven; but I think it is a reasonable thing to fright persons away from hell." While probably overemphasizing hell, Edwards was seeking to bring men and women to an awareness of and response to the love of God in Christ. Thus his ultimate motivation was of a much higher nature than is commonly supposed.

It has always been hard to keep a balance between the prophetic foretelling of bad news and the foretelling of good news. The author of 2 Esdras in the Apocrypha envisions the last day as primarily an event of doom for the sinful rather than victory for the righteous. A case in point is to be found in his closing remarks:

> Alas for those who are bound by their sins and covered with their wickedness, as a field is overgrown with woods, and its grain so covered with thorns that no one can get through. It is shut out, and left to be consumed by fire (6:77–78).

Many artists of orthodox vintage have overstressed hell as did Michelangelo in his judgment scene in the Sistine Chapel where one's eyes are riveted on the lost on the *left* of Christ.

The razor edge of divine truth is so thin as to leave most thinkers on one side or the other. Motivation to evangelize is usually an excessive emphasis on the place of *gehenna* in the concept of mission or an almost total neglect of the doctrine. Belief in hell was a prime motive in the Early Church for the saving of men. The later evangelizing of pagan nations around the globe was largely brought about by men like William Carey, Adoniram Judson, and David Livingstone who felt the urgency to snatch the natives from hell. Those who came out of the Haystack Prayer Meeting in Massachusetts were convinced that the unregenerate are destined for *gehenna,* thus the Christian church had no need for further orders. The gospel of salvation had to be preached to *all* men. Failing to fulfill the Great Commission meant that the Christian himself would bear the responsibility for the damnation of the lost. Isaac Watts would have agreed since, for him at least, the proclamation of the eternal terrors of hell

> . . . seems to be the appointed and most effectual way to rouse their [the wicked] consciences to seek a deliverance from the curses of the law, which carry in them everlasting punishment.—*The World to Come*, p. 431

A well-known contemporary evangelist, Alan Walker of Australia, would strongly question the legitimacy of Watt's conviction. While he would not seek to annul the validity of the preaching of hell in the eighteenth century, the contemporary evangelist would insist that such a concept is fruitless today.

> The motive, the urgency for mission, must today be re-expressed. After all, the older motive for evangelism has largely died. Whence came that former urgency? From belief in hell. The picture was simple. Men and women, unless reconciled to God in Christ by the moment of death, fell into the tortures of hell, from which there was no escape. . . . This belief has gone. Even where ideas of an everlasting hell linger, the eternal consequences of the rejection of Christ are proclaimed with muted voice.—*A Ringing Call to Mission*, p. 14

We must admit that the proclamation of hell is heard only faintly if at all in modern times. Some churchmen are casting aside any and all eschatological (end time) concepts as they relate to evangelism. Not only is the subject of hell abandoned but that of heaven as well. If the wicked are to be evangelized in the last half of the twentieth century, we are told that it is to be done only within the framework of an existential (present time) theology. It is this present world which is important, not a world to come. The so-called new evangelism is almost totally dedicated to changing the social, political, and economic structures of society. The late D. T. Niles of Ceylon states:

> The evangelistic concern is not with the question as to
> how Christ will deal hereafter with those who in this life
> have not found faith in him: its concern is simply with the
> fact that now he calls men to repent and to perform deeds
> worthy of their repentance.—*The Preacher's Task and the
> Stone of Stumbling,* p. 34

Regardless as to how one may feel about the balance between
the vision of men *dying* without Christ and *living* without Him,
we cannot ignore the fact that Jesus had a good bit to say about
the end of the age. While He did not give us many details about
what lies beyond the grave, His concern about the end implies
His interest in what follows. For us to be indifferent to this
dimension of the Biblical record is synonymous with refusing to
present the whole gospel. It is also to treat the concerns of Jesus
with despite.

Advocates of universalism and its related theories do not reject evangelism *in toto*. Rather evangelism is reinterpreted to
mean the expression of love for one's neighbor. This is perfectly consistent if it is impossible or unlikely that any man could
be finally lost. The Biblical urgency, which rested on eschatology,
is lessened by either a universalist or an existential persuasion.
Thus the substitute motivation becomes a desire to introduce
men to Christ in order that their lives may be bettered while on
the earth. *This is certainly a part of the Christian message but it
is not all.* And we should never forget that the best *neighbor* is
he who saves a man from hell as well as aids him in finding the
good life here!

It is often argued by churchmen of such theological stance as
that described above that preaching about the future has little
effect on men who are primarily concerned with living in the
present. There is a point for this side of the ledger, though ad-
mittedly a weak one, in the gospel itself. J. Henry Cadbury points
out that when the rich man asked for a messenger from the
other world to be sent to his surviving brothers to warn them,
he was told,

"If they do not hear Moses and the prophets neither will they be convinced if some one should rise from the dead." . . . According to this word, so surprisingly for any early Christian document, reformed conduct in this life would not be promoted by more convincing evidence of the future life or judgment.—*Immortality and Resurrection*, p. 145

In spite of the insinuation that discoursing upon the life to come has little to do with modern man, there have been times when men were genuinely moved toward God by the thought of what will follow this existence in time. Whether man is essentially different from what he was a generation or a century ago is a question as yet unresolved.

The world is different, but there seems to be something stable about the inner life of man in every age. We may be incorrect in speaking of "modern man" as though all men in this age are alike. Perhaps, some are motivated by confrontation with thoughts of life after death and others are not regardless as to what period in history we are studying. Watts writes of people in the nineteenth century as though they were all alike in his day. It is clearly obvious that they were not, though what he states was probably generally true.

It is confessed that a discourse on this dreadful subject hell is not a direct ministration of grace and the glad tidings of salvation, yet it has a great and happy tendency to the same end, even the salvation of sinful men. It awakens them to a more piercing sight, and to a more keen sensation of their own guilt and danger; it possesses their spirits with a more lively sense of their misery; it fills them with a holy dread of divine punishment, and excites the powerful passion of fear to make them fly from the wrath to come, and betake themselves to the grace of God revealed in the Gospel.—*The World to Come*, p. 355

A good bit of debate continues to revolve around the validity of this "fear motivation" which appears to have dominated the first eighteen hundred years of Christian evangelism. It is true that men will act when frightened, but such action is believed to be superficial and temporary. While it is argued that the preacher's most effective weapon is that of fear, it must be acknowledged that there is far more in the God-man relationship than fear to bind us together. F. B. Edge is saying much the same thing when he writes,

> It would probably be accurate to say that the fundamental motive that lies at the center of the average church member's "decision for Christ" is the desire to escape the "horrors of hell" and share in the "joys of heaven." Of course, man lives in the hope of eternal life. This is no small part of the Christian experience. It is a worthy and valid hope. But when the hope of heaven constitutes the whole of one's religious experience, there is reason to question whether he has entered into a genuine saving relationship.—*A Quest for Vitality in Religion*, p. 169

The utopia of the Kingdom of God would be found in a discipleship which springs from motives which are wholly unselfish. Whether such motivation can ever be found in anyone's life is a sticky question. The witch of Alexandria was not practicing very *black* magic when, carrying a burning fagot and a pitcher of water through the streets of Athens, she expressed a desire to damp the fires of hell and set fire to heaven so that man would love God for Himself alone. Most likely, however, man will always have to be dealt with as he exists.

There are numerous motivating levels in every person and evangelism is most successful when it is flexible enough to start with man where he is. Paul Buchanan charts these motivating levels in a graphic continuum which moves from the lower motivation of physiological needs to the highest motivation of self-actualization (*The Leader and Individual Motivation*, p. 45). To put it another way, man moves on levels which may be primitive or unenlightened. He may also be motivated at various periods of his life at differing levels between these extremes. Evangelism which employs the proclamation of hell does so because such doctrine is believed to be true and further because the thought of judgment is the initial sign of religion in unredeemed men.

Some have argued that the use of *gehenna* in the mission of the church is a threat. Others look at its use differently. Donald Bloesch feels that "one will not strive to work out his salvation in fear and trembling if there is no divine judgment in the future, if there is no threat of condemnation" (*Crisis of Piety*, p. 42). Such persons feel that a Biblical, compassionate, and concerned presentation of the doctrine might better be described as preventive discipline. In this sense, the preaching and teaching of *gehenna* would serve the same purpose as having an understanding with one's own children. Jonathan Edwards speaks to this matter in *The Distinguishing Marks*.

> If any of you who are heads of families saw one of your children in a house all on fire, and in imminent danger of being consumed in the flames, yet seemed to be very insensible of its danger, and neglected to escape after you had called to it—would you go on to speak to it only in a cold indifferent manner? Would you not cry aloud, and call earnestly to it, and represent the danger it was in, and its own folly in delaying, in the most lively manner of which you were capable?

Advocates of the use of the doctrine of hell in evangelism believe that preventive discipline is necessary if one is to avoid the ultimate consequences of disobedience. It is insisted that there are inexorable laws which one needs to be apprised of early lest the latter state be an awakening to bitter and unavoidable punitive judgment. Marshall McLuhan writes,

> As Gospel salesmen, remember that you are selling something that most people are terrified of. . . . The Gospel has long been sold by the aid of very bad news, namely hell fire. And I think we're going to find that an indispensable dimension of it. . . . Christ never failed to harp on that note. And I think you'll find that you're not going to sell very much Gospel without a lot of bad news.—*Christianity Today*, February 13, 1970

In speaking of the wrath of God, which is the back side of His love, a contemporary in the field of evangelism writes,

> That is an element of theology which is of immense importance to the evangelist. It must be handled with care, for it would be fatally easy to make an unethical use of it. But it supplies a sanction that for far too long has been conspicuous by its absence in evangelistic preaching. We should not be afraid to utilize both the demand of the law and the penalties of judgment in urging the claims of the Gospel.—A. SKEVINGTON WOOD, *Evangelism—Its Theology and Practice,* p. 36

Is the urgency for evangelism adequate without the concept of *gehenna?* Will the evangelist be as compelled to seek men for the Kingdom if he is convinced that they cannot be lost? And will the outsider feel as constrained to change his life unless there is some awareness of possible ultimate loss? These are questions which have to be considered. And they are sobering enough to disturb even an atheist who wrote in derision:

> Did I firmly believe, as millions say they do, that the knowledge and practice of religion in this life influences destiny in another . . . I should esteem one soul gained for heaven worth a life of suffering. Earthly consequences should never stay my hand, nor seal my lips. Earth, its joys and its griefs, would occupy no moment of my thoughts. I would strive to look upon eternity alone and on the immortal souls around me, soon to be everlastingly happy or everlastingly miserable. I would go forth to the world and preach it in season and out of season, and my text would be "what shall it profit a man if he gain the whole world and lose his soul?"—NORMAN GRUBB, *C. T. Studd,* p. 40

Billy Graham tells of a delegate to the World Council of Churches who informed the division on evangelism that a new evangelistic urgency is needed, that the church can no longer employ the idea of hell. Dr. Graham commented that he thought there was something left to be said for hell!

The urgency which prompts anxious correctives for the world's problems of nuclear energy, race, and ecology is based on a fear of destruction. Why should this be good motivation when preaching on hell is bad motivation? Some insist that the motive is "brotherhood." It is possible that this may be only a part of it. The motivations are mixed as in evangelism where both the *love* of Christ and our brothers and the *fear* of hell are involved. No one would question the wisdom of emphasizing the invitation of God as a loving Father who waits to forgive and redeem those who come to Him in repentance and faith. But neither can we be considered wise unless we remind the world that a rejection of that invitation will result in eternal separation and loss.

Discussion Questions for Chapter 7

1. *Would you consider the idea of hell a low or high level of motivation? How could it be used wrongly?*
2. *What danger do you see in the use of this doctrine by evangelists with selfish objectives? Can it be used to manipulate? How?*
3. *Is our motivation to evangelize and carry out the Great Commission lessened today because of the long neglect of a concentration on hell? Do the unregenerate feel less inclination to seek salvation when they are not warned about the consequences of being lost?*
4. *Explain how our contemporary understanding of evangelism as changing the social order militates against the doctrine of hell. How it contributes to it.*
5. *What place can be found in today's existential situation for serious reflection on life after death? Judgment and hell?*
6. *How can the idea of hell be a threat? How can it be a preventive? Can it be used in any other way?*
7. *Is the church being unfaithful to Christ and unfair with men in its abandonment of the doctrine of hell? Suggest how this might be corrected.*

8

Today's Evangelism and the Forgotten Concept

As early as 1929 G. M. Betts insisted that the ultimate fate of the wicked was scarcely dealt with by ministers, writers, theologians, or seminaries (*The Beliefs of 700 Ministers*, pp. 24–61). This radical shift in theological perspective may have developed due to a number of causes, some of which follow.

1. The rise of Biblical or higher criticism which sought to distrust anything which did not fit into the rationalistic mold which was formed by theologians of a scientific bent.

2. A reaction to the extreme way in which the doctrine of hell had been proclaimed by some in the past.

3. The advance of humanitarianism which decried any idea of God which made Him less gracious than a good man who would not damn anyone.

The outcome of such rationalization is described by R. W. Gleason when he writes:

Sentimentality, secular humanism, and determinism have produced their own bitter fruit: the defiling of the sense of the transcendent majesty of God, and of the inescapable responsibility of man's moral choices. It is no longer generally believed, to put the matter bluntly, that man is capable of choices that could bring him to eternal death.
—*The World to Come*, p. 114

Gleason has added the influence of behavioral psychology to the reasons for the almost complete neglect of the Biblical doctrine of hell. The determinists have convinced modern man that he is not really responsible for anything that he does. The environmental (and hereditary) factors in the world around him have so shaped his life that the average man has simply responded to the stimuli beyond his own control. If he is not responsible there is no such thing as sin. And if there is no sin there is no guilt. Therefore, the whole idea of future punishment in hell is so ridiculous as to have become a laughing matter. What man does is due to the way he was made plus the accident which placed him in one environment rather than another. He is a machine, programmed by his surroundings and continually reinforced in his attitudes and actions by the culture of which he is a part.

Modern man, with all his sophisticated knowledge, has advanced very little beyond the religious views of the ancients. The most primitive man believed that destiny was out of his hands. The gods determined everything and man had nothing to do with it except to try to get by one day at a time without being destroyed by the angry gods. Even the Stoics of New Testament times (learned men who lived in one of history's most advanced intellectual climates) were so sure that Providence determined everything that they saw no reason to even discuss their destiny. In our day, the idea of God's having determined our existence does not occur to most of us because we have decided that there may not even be any God. We do accept the notion that our destinies are fixed by impersonal forces outside ourselves. Thus we become obsessed by the here and now and refuse to worry about a future which we cannot change or which may never come. With such a philosophy as this, why worry about hell?

Most of our preaching and teaching today is directed toward moral improvement rather than divine judgment and mercy. It is no wonder that the Christian church seems so weak and ineffective in the modern world. If the moral improvement of man is all there is to this business of religion it is possible that the secular world can do about as well as those within the church. In fact, even the word *moral* could be removed from most descriptions of what the church is about. Our objective is sheer improvement as though mankind can lift itself by its own bootstraps. Our religious life is almost wholly earthbound and the warnings of Jesus about what follows this interval in time are given little or no attention.

Christian leaders appear to be practically helpless, unable to even talk about the ultimate result of unresolved guilt. Only in the most fundamentalistic branches of the church does one even hear the word *hell* mentioned. Those who dare to accept such a notion as everlasting punishment are classified as narrow and unenlightened. They are brushed aside by the so-called more respectable clergy and laity as not having read the latest theological views. They are just not in-the-know. Such people are reminded that "we must at once throw over as unworthy of God any vestigial ideas remaining in our minds that anyone, whatever he believes or does, is landed in some kind of endless torture after death (Weatherhead, *The Christian Agnostic*, p. 281).

The most popular concept of our times which seeks to deny the doctrine of hell is that of universalism. Pink dogmatically affirms that "the very fact that universalism is so popular with the wicked is proof irresistible that it is not the system taught in the Bible" (Arthur Pink, *Eternal Punishment*, p. 7). Certainly, this observation is in keeping with the tone of the New Testament which affirms that the popular path is the *broad* way that leads to hell. The Catholic theologian, Georges Panneton, finds this idea of universalism as repugnant as does Pink.

> Liberal Protestants are reviving another heresy of Origen . . . which denies the eternity of Hell. "One day," they say, "God will close Hell, and make peace with the demons and damned." We call these heretics *universalists,* because they would have universal salvation, at the expense of the justice and holiness of God.—*Heaven or Hell,* p. 199

Arguing for universalism as a substitute for *gehenna* is Weatherhead who states, "The consummation of the age will mean that both the condition we have called hell and that which we have called heaven will pass away, and give place to a new condition, when the perfect life begins" (*After Death,* 64, 65). The only trouble with this kind of rationalizing is that it is not even remotely akin to what the Bible teaches. Lewis Dunnington is fully as convinced that at least hell will have an end.

> We can bear punishment, either for ourselves or for others, only if we believe it will achieve an end that makes suffering worth-while. If hell is endless, it is valueless, since its victims would never have a chance of repenting and becoming good.—*Power to Become,* p. 223

Again, there is nothing wrong with this kind of teaching except that it is not what Jesus said. What the Christian has to decide once and for all is who he is going to listen to—Christ and those who agree with what He taught, or those who prefer to teach something concocted in the philosophical circles of a humanistic church. We would be hardhearted indeed if we did not have the deep hope that the universalists are right and we are wrong. Such hope has so little (if any) scriptural support, however, that we dare not trust so lighthearted and irresponsible a doctrine.

The late William Sangster (of Central Hall of Methodism in London) believed man must be responsible for his own destiny if he is to be free to choose. His observations appear to us to be much more firmly rooted in the Biblical record:

> If man's freedom is real, he is free to turn from God and persist in the direction he has chosen. If God forces himself on no one (because he respects the freedom which he has given), even those of us most aware of the love of God must concede the possibility that some will resist that love and be lost. Some devout Christians . . . nourish the hope that all will ultimately be saved. But . . . they know that, if God compelled people to accept him, he would be treating them as "things" and not as persons. . . . So let us remember that hell is not a fitting subject for jokes, nor yet to be waived airily aside on the ground that God is a "gentleman" who will overlook everything at the last. He made us

free; and we are free, if we choose, to be damned.—*Questions People Ask About Religion*, pp. 131, 132

One of the most impassioned repudiations of universalism by a modern scholar who is vitally concerned about the restoration of Biblical theology, reads:

One of the most pernicious theories to beset Christianity is that of universalism, which holds that all men will ultimately be saved. Although some biblical and philosophical arguments can be brought forward to support this position, surely the whole tenor of Christ's teaching is against it.— HAROLD BROWN, *The Protest of a Troubled Protestant*, p. 110

While it is obvious that the preaching of hellfire-and-brimstone does not occupy a conspicuously large place in either theological disputes or the proclamation of the Good News from the pulpits, it remains a fact that more concern with the doctrine of hell exists among us than is usually recognized. A contemporary professor from the West Coast has carefully observed the modern scene and found this to be true.

Recently I attended a clinic on the James Kennedy plan of evangelism and was simply stunned to find how grateful people were for those who talked to them earnestly and openly about ultimate matters of faith and life. In one of my seminary classes, some forty students are going out weekly in visitation evangelism. They are returning with the same experience. People want to talk about God, life, death, heaven, hell, the future of the world, and the amazing fact that God loves them as they are.—ROBERT MUNGER, *Eternity*, August, 1971

What is just as amazing as the "fact that God loves them" is the fact that the masses are anxious to hear about hell as well as heaven, judgment as well as love. They are even rather disinterested in the theological conflict between divine judgment and love. This does not seem to bother them at all. Especially is this true among informed laymen within the church, that is, the desire to hear more about the ultimate issues of life and death. The following letter from a leading layman in the northeast is a case in point.

It has been a long time since I have heard any reference to Gehenna or Hell in a Methodist Church. It's as though this word or concept has just dropped out of sight. When questions are asked most ministers avoid any direct answer and a few state that regardless of what Jesus said, there is no such place. The layman is confused for, though Jesus was very specific about Hell and made several references to it, his minister avoids it and Methodist literature seldom mentions it.

For some years now, the popular answer to Hell is that the place is only symbolic and doesn't exist. A God of love would certainly never condemn anyone to such a horrible fate and Jesus must have been using colorful language and exaggeration to make a point. This answer is comforting and reassuring but I believe that the Christian message has been severely weakened by this non-scriptural approach and this may be one of the most important reasons for the dropping off of evangelical zeal by Methodist laymen.

If there really is no such place as Hell and somehow all people will be saved by a loving God, then what's the hurry? Why go to all that trouble if it doesn't really make too much difference when others accept Christ?

Because I believe that the Bible is the Word of God and divinely inspired, I accept what it says as being true. Hell is mentioned often and Jesus makes specific references to it. Therefore, whether or not I like it or understand it, I believe it. Since coming to this conclusion, I find I have a much stronger motivation to evangelize. Though I cannot describe Hell or even justify it, I know that it's a place I never want to be nor do I want any of my loved ones or friends to go there.

I believe that God is love and this is primary to our Christian faith. However, the Bible tells us that He is also just and there will be a Day of Judgment. This element of God cannot be overlooked and Jesus speaks clearly to this issue.

Hell is obviously a place to be avoided. I don't believe that Jesus' death on the cross was only to save us from ourselves, or to make life a pleasure here on earth. If so, it was an awful price to pay for such a small prize.

Our evangelistic mission in the Church should be to go forth in love to tell the Good News. In telling the story, we must tell it all, like it really is according to Jesus. If men and women deny Jesus and offend God, then they face a life in Hell after death. If we believe this then we must do all we can to see that everyone believes it.

If the Methodist laity felt that all of their loved ones, relatives, friends, and acquaintances who do not know Christ were going to face the Hell that Jesus describes, they would really mobilize to get the Good News out and before the people.

We have been remiss for too long. Our soft, loving approach with no consequences has failed to convert the unbeliever. Why not tell the whole story? After all, Jesus included it and discussed it. Can we do any less? At the risk of offending, we must tell the truth. Maybe evangelism will be born again as a dynamic thrust of the Church if we give the nonbeliever the opportunity to hear the whole story—not just the part of it we like.—GEORGE E. CURTIS

Some of the world's most prominent theologians have not thrown away the concept of hell. The futuristic element is the warp and woof of the gospel message and its built-in motivation, according to Joachim Jeremias. He wisely notes

. . . the perpetual twofold issue of all preaching of the gospel: the offer of mercy and the threat of impending judgment inseparable from it, deliverance and fear, salvation and destruction, life and death.—*The Message of the Parable of Jesus*, p. 18

Jeremias continues, later in the same book on page 226 where he comments on the twin parables of the tares and the fish:

God has fixed the moment of separation. The measure of time assigned by Him must be fulfilled . . . , the seed must be allowed to ripen. Then comes the end, and with it the separation between tares and wheat, the sorting out of the fish, with the dividing of good fish from bad.

Another contemporary theologian, holding the traditional Roman Catholic doctrine of hell, is Georges Panneton who writes:

> There is only the one choice, Heaven or Hell, eternal happiness or eternal misery. When we come to the end of our lives, we have to make that choice, every one of us without exception. Better by far to do it now, so as to be prepared, for death can come upon us very suddenly.
>
> Often we get a wrong view of things by looking upon a man as the center upon which the world revolves. We must come back to the theocentric ideas: man, like all other creatures, was created by God, and wisdom dictates that he should glorify God by one or the other way: in happiness or in misery, whichever he himself has chosen.—*Heaven or Hell,* pp. 7, 8 and 236

Georgia Harkness sounds somewhat like this latter statement of Panneton when she exclaims:

> Eternal life . . . is not simply continuance after death; it is a quality of life which begins here and is endless. Because this is true, can we not then assume that the rejection of the call to love and serve God lies also on *both* sides of death? Hell in this life is certainly a reality; there is no sufficient reason to think that it ends with death.—*Beliefs That Count,* p. 114

John S. Bonnell joins Miss Harkness in stating, "No man will experience an outward hell who has not felt its beginnings in his own heart. Hell has its commencement in the here and now" (*Heaven and Hell,* p. 41).

Altizer, proponent of the now defunct God-is-dead theology, ponders a question which must have some real validity when he states, "Is it because the Church can no longer speak about Hell and damnation that we hear so much foolish ecclesiastical clatter about forgiveness? What can an ultimate forgiveness mean if it is impossible to speak about an ultimate guilt?" (*The Gospel of Christian Atheism*, p. 140). Emil Brunner has questions, too, but he tends to fade into ambiguity when he attempts to argue both for universalism and damnation while admitting that the two doctrines "are not logically compatible." He concludes on a teeter-totter by suggesting:

> All "symmetrical" logically satisfying knowledge of God is fatal. Therefore the criterion of all true theology is this, that it should conclude with the words "God be merciful to me a sinner" (Luke 18:13) and over and above that with this other word: "But thanks be to God which giveth us the victory through our Lord Jesus Christ" (1 Corinthians 15:57).—*The Christian Doctrine of the Church, Faith, and the Consummation*, III, pp. 423, 424

The Swiss theologian's solution to the parable in Matthew 25:31–46 (the sheep and the goats) is to see the parable as shattering self-assurance and offering salvation as a possibility for all (*Eternal Hope*, p. 182). A. Motyer insists that the message of the parable is something else entirely:

> Three things seem clear: first, that on the day of judgment it will not be a matter of God's summoning people to repent, but of His declaring what their state before Him is; it will be a day of pronouncing, not inviting. Secondly, the parable seems to teach that the decision of that Court settles matters eternally. Thirdly, there will be a division and not all will be saved.—*After Death*, p. 29

We will probably do well here to point out that the parable of the sheep and the goats, which has been referred to several times in the discussion, is hardly ever interpreted properly. The burden of the Messianic teaching in this parable has to do with the separation of the *nations* at the end time. The sheep and the goats represent nations rather than individuals (though nations are comprised of individuals and it is hard to distinguish one

from the other). When Jesus makes the acceptance or rejection
of the nations (the Gentiles) dependent upon their treatment of
"these my brethren" He is referring to the Jewish people. The
Jews were uniquely His *brethren*. Since the time of Abraham
God had promised that the nations of the world would either
bless themselves or curse themselves by the manner in which
they treated His chosen people (Genesis 12:1–3). Ultimately, in a
discussion of *gehenna*, regardless as to whether one interprets
this parable correctly as having to do with the Jewish nation or
incorrectly as relating to people in general, the final results for
the wicked are the same. Thus, Motyer is right in his three observations.

After a lengthy, penetrating examination of the evidence, C.
Ryder Smith draws a definite conclusion: "To the present writer
it seems impossible, if the evidence is considered objectively, to
deny that there is a doctrine of 'everlasting punishment' in the
New Testament" (*The Bible Doctrine of the Hereafter*, p. 220).

After explaining the reasons for not understanding *aionios* in
Matthew 25 to mean *everlasting*, D. P. Walker suggests that such
an interpretation is unlikely "since Christ is clearly drawing a
parallel between the eternity of bliss awaiting the sheep and the
eternity of misery awaiting the goats. It can only stand if one
also denies eternal life to the saved" (*Decline of Hell*, pp. 19, 20).
Merrill F. Unger is likewise certain of the consequences of evil
in the world to come: "Of the fact of future punishment and of
the eternal duration in some form the teachings of Christ and the
apostles leave no room for doubt" (*Unger's Bible Dictionary*, p.
901). A Wesleyan work agrees with Unger's study when com-
menting on Mark 9:43–47 (the remark of Jesus about excising
troublous members):

> This is a terrible description of eternal torment. It should
> be noted that these strongest warnings against the horrors
> of hell fell from the lips of the supposedly "meek and mild
> Jesus." The "gentle Galilean" could and did speak out with
> unforgettable sternness about the eternal consequences of
> sin. One had better lose everything in this life than lose his

soul forever in hell.—*The Wesleyan Bible Commentary*, IV, p. 166

One of the youngest theological scholars to deal with the question of hell is Harold O. J. Brown. Deeply disturbed over the loss of concepts in theology which he feels to be basic to the faith, Brown writes,

> In a strange way, hell is necessary for human significance. If no man, no matter what he did, could finally rebel against God, but all men were ultimately to be brought back into harmony with God through a kind of irresistible grace, then all the moral and spiritual struggles of men would have no more meaning, in the last analysis, than the wrigglings of hamsters in a laboratory cage.—*The Protest of a Troubled Protestant*, p. 110

It has been erroneously believed that interest in the study of hell is restricted to the field of evangelism and that only a few of those doing serious investigation in this area are interested at all. On the contrary, even from the world of religious education, scholars are adding their positive word to the concept of hell in the mission of the church. Indeed, the mission of Christianity cannot be departmentalized but is integrally involved with every area of church life. Miller says, "The essential meaning of Hell, whether here or hereafter, is exclusion from fellowship with God, and the essential meaning of Heaven is the experience of that fellowship" (Randolph C. Miller, *The Clue to Christian Education*, pp. 190, 191). F. B. Edge is as fully convinced when he observes, "If God was willing to make the supreme sacrifice of His Son on the cross for man's redemption, is it not reasonable to suppose that the 'final end' of man 'out of Christ' (however it may be described) is desperate in nature?" (*A Quest for Vitality in Religion*, p. 150).

There are some within the Christian fellowship who still concern themselves about the fundamentals of the faith. In our day we are despised and laughed at if we dare to affirm that the cardinal teachings of the New Testament Church are still apropos to us and binding on our creed. Yet some dare to stand erect in the face of the advancing tide of humanism. Herschel H. Hobbs must be credited as one of the braver proponents of fundamental Christian truth.

> As heaven is more wonderful than symbols can picture it, so hell is more terrible than its symbols describe it. If hell is not fire, it is something infinitely worse. No wonder Jesus warned against it so often and so emphatically! No wonder that God paid such a price to save men from it!—*Fundamentals of Our Faith,* p. 146

> Many people deny the existence of hell. Yet Jesus said more about hell than he did about heaven. Such denial is due more to wishful thinking and sentimental reasoning than to an interpretation of the factual teaching of the Bible. To say that a merciful God would not make a hell is to examine only one facet of God's nature. He is love. But He is holiness and righteousness also. God sends no one to hell. Each person goes there of his own will despite all that God in Christ has done to prevent it.—*What Baptists Believe,* pp. 116, 117

The breeding ground for scholars who find ways to annul the clear teachings of the Bible has been, at least for half a century, in the institutions of higher learning in Germany. Yet, one of the world's leading pastor-theologians to have come to the forefront since World War II is the German scholar, Helmut Thielicke. From the midst of colleagues who stand among the Bible's most severe critics, Thielicke writes:

> . . . to be in hell simply means to be utterly separated from God, but in such a way that one is compelled to see him, that one must see him as a thirsty man sees a silvery spring from which he dare not drink. This is hell: to be forced to see the glory of God and have no access to it. . . . The opposite of eternal rest and security is to be compelled to endure that state in which everything is forfeited forever. . . . —*The Waiting Father,* p. 48

It should be recalled at this point that the rich man in Jesus' story recorded by Luke was able to see into the bosom of Abraham where Lazarus enjoyed the blessings of the world to come. The rich man was in torments and, in view of his miserable state and that of Lazarus's joyous one, he wanted to warn others about hell's horrors. To see what we have missed and know that it is no longer obtainable is hell indeed!

The one evangelist's voice heard by more people than any other one churchman in history, speaks clearly and forcefully in support of the view which sees hell as separation from God. Billy Graham admits, "I can't pretend to solve all the mysteries of hell, but whatever else hell may mean, it is separation from God. Jesus used three words to describe it: 'fire,' 'darkness,' and 'death' " (*Decision,* September, 1969). While not in complete agreement with the above reference, Pannenberg shares the concept of separation:

> The pictorial value of the conceptions of internal torment must be judged inadequate, since the decisive factor, exclusion from God, does not appear among the images of the bottomless pit. This is precisely the only element of the conceptions of hell that theology must retain and set free from fantastic incrustations. To be excluded from God's nearness in spite of clear consciousness of it would be hell.—*Jesus, God and Man,* pp. 270, 271

No one speaks more poignantly about hell as separation from God than does the distinguished English rector of All Souls Church in London.

> Hell is a grim and dreadful reality. Let no man deceive you. Jesus himself spoke of it. He called it "outer darkness" because it is an infinite separation from God who is light. It is also called in the Bible "the second death" and "the lake of fire," terms which describe symbolically the forfeiture of eternal life and the ghastly thirst of the soul which are involved in irrevocable banishment from God's presence.—JOHN R. W. STOTT, *Basic Christianity,* p. 73

A popular young Presbyterian preacher says in a sermon on the rich man and Lazarus in Luke 19,

> Where did hell come from? God didn't do it in the Apostles' Creed. Dives dug his share, day after day, inch by erosive inch, drip by drip, until by his accumulated indifference and divergent interest, he had alienated himself from God by a Grand Canyon's worth. Dives had been learning, practicing all his life, how to live on "the wrong side of the sky." . . . Dives had had his chance and it was gone—forever.—DAVID REDDING, *The Parables He Told,* p. 153

It is true that Dives was in *hades* and not *gehenna* (see chapter 1, but Jesus made it clear that his condition was permanent. Redding, therefore, is correct in his statement about the duration of punishment on the basis of this instance in Scripture.

H. N. Hancock argues that, if men are free, then each one "must be free to choose, not only where he will spend a two-week summer vacation, but whether he will spend eternity with God, which is Heaven, or without Him, which is Hell" (*And After This,* p. 97). The editors of the world's most widely-circulated evangelical Christian journal provide a fitting summation of the basic view as understood by their reading public.

> Scripture seems to say to men: Choose whom you will serve, but know what the consequences of your choice will be. A righteous God whose holiness has been offended could not remain righteous if he did not pass judgment on stubborn, unrepentant sinners, who have confirmed themselves in their wicked ways. Having been warned of the consequences of their sins, men cannot blame God if he confirms in them for eternity what they have confirmed in themselves in this life.—*Christianity Today,* November 20, 1970, p. 34

While it may be considered commendable to be flexible and academically wise to be uncommitted to a dogmatic position on the doctrine of hell, there are some who believe that such an ambiguous approach is at least unfortunate for the church. "The question now is," according to Ralph Turnbull, are we missing a breakthrough in communication because we hesitate to use the eschatological approach and motif?" (*The Preacher's Heritage, Task, and Resources,* p. 104).

The Puritans were opposed to the old practice of bear-baiting not so much due to the pain experienced by the bear as to the pleasure it brought to the hunter. And, though we cannot share their suspicion of anything which brought enjoyment, their objection to pleasure in another's misery, whether man or beast, was commendable. Satan's traps are set and the bait is out. Multitudes will be snared by the adversary and destroyed. No Christian can ever take delight in the wicked's getting his due. But neither can he fail to love him enough to warn him of his plight. We must all go forth with weeping, bearing the warning of everlasting punishment in hell and the offer of eternal life in heaven.

Is it possible that the message of the modern church has no more bite to it than gums from which the teeth have been extracted? In our intent to offset the extremes of some earlier and cruder presentations of divine judgment, have we shown to the world an emasculated gospel? With the teeth all gone, does the proclamation seem a bit too soft and sentimental for a rough-tough-and-tumble world like we have today? And is it possible that preaching itself has gone into partial eclipse because it has failed to deal honestly with the whole gospel? If there is anything which the younger generation demands of the church, it is that we be honest with them!

A Hindu once demanded that E. Stanley Jones convert him. It was a strange approach. When the famous missionary asked for further explanation, the Hindu swore that unless Jones converted him he would sue him. And when asked on what grounds such drastic action would be taken, the Christian missionary was told "on breach of promise." In reality, the Hindu was right since being a Christian is its own promise to be an agent of divine redemption. Manifestly, it is the Holy Spirit who does the converting, not man. But every Christian is innately endowed with a measure of that Spirit and commissioned by the Lord Himself

to go "to all peoples everywhere and make them my disciples
. . ." (Matthew 28:19 TEV).

To do what Christ has commanded it is compulsory that we be
motivated. The fact that men are lost and destined for eternal
punishment if they live and die without Christ is a valid part of
that motivation. Indeed, if neglect of the eternal salvation of a
world for which we are responsible were a matter subject to a
court of law, those of us who do not "save a soul from death"
(James 5:20) could be sued. And since justice cannot be granted
to the unsaved against the unconcerned Christian here, the
settlement at the final judgment may be stiffer than can now be
imagined.

A part of the urgency which accompanies the preaching of the
gospel is surely to be found in this divine wrath upon disobedience. If we understand this and still do nothing about warning
the lost, we cannot be said to be worthy channels for the communication of the gospel of redemption.

Discussion Questions for Chapter 8

1. *Recalling the discussion of behavioral science as it relates to
   man's sense of guilt, explain how determinism seeks to throw
   out the Christian doctrine of hell as punishment for sin.*
2. *Describe how the modern church might go about restoring
   the doctrine of hell to its proper place in a society where
   religion has become almost exclusively "this-worldly."*
3. *Universalism is a growing heresy in our day. What measures
   could be employed to offset this growth and refute such indoc-
   trination?*
4. *How are we to interpret the fact that informed laymen, especially young people, indicate a desire to hear about judgment
   and hell at the very time when theologians and many clergymen are denying these Biblical truths?*
5. *If there is no hell because man is not guilty, what does this do
   to the Christian message of divine forgiveness for the sinner?*
6. *In what way does "final and irrevocable separation from God"*

describe the basic meaning of hell? Does this idea fall short of giving the full picture? How?

7. In the event that the Christian church fails to proclaim the whole counsel of God, which includes clear teaching on hell, who will be apt to experience the reality of hell most—the unfaithful church or the unrepentant world?

9

The Essence of Hell

The writer's intent has been to present an objective investigation of a topic almost universally ignored. If at times a subjective bias shows through, it has been unintentional. The effort to produce a completely objective study is hardly ever 100 percent successful. Each person brings certain presuppositions to an investigation which color everything that he reads or writes. Such hues and tints uncovered by the reader are incidental to the purpose of this study. We have done our best to be objectively honest. It is not uncommon for the reader to find biases which are not actually existent because of the personal bias which he himself brings to the perusal. Caution will need to be taken at this point by those who study this book. The question which must be asked at each juncture in the mental pilgrimage is whether the conclusions arrived at by the writer are borne out by the Biblical record.

Throughout the examination of the concept of hell in the evangelistic mission of the church, we have been impressed by several things. First is the scarcity of recent or contemporary writing and preaching on the subject. During the first eighteen hundred years of the Christian era the church was almost obsessed with the joys of heaven and the horrors of hell. Since that time interest has waned until, following World War II, hardly anything of serious consequence has been undertaken in the field. One is fortunate occasionally to find a paragraph or even a sentence in a theological work or a printed sermon which relates directly to the subject of hell. The investigator is doubly blessed if he discovers a whole chapter or even several pages in any kind of writing. With rare exception, the churchgoer can attend worship for years without ever hearing a word about hell. The scarcity of materials gives us our first clue that the subject of hell is taboo in many quarters and ignored in others.

A second impression relates to the manner in which the views on hell are presented. The more dominant treatment among theologians and scholastic preachers is to reinterpret hell in a framework which offers a second chance after death, embraces some kind of universalism, or simply casts out the whole idea as outdated. Annihilation does not seem to have as strong a following as we might expect, though it is by no means a dead issue. Eternal punishment is hardly ever considered a live option and, when it is, the concept is expounded with muted voice. If this latter interpretation is defended it is on the basis of the inspiration and authority of the Bible. Persons who believe in the doctrine of eternal punishment feel strongly about it. Their numbers are just not as great as they once were.

Primarily, the reason for negation of hell as eternal torment is based on the nature of God which John says is love. It is argued that God cannot be both a God of love and a capricious, sadistic tormentor of men. Furthermore, it is insisted that everlasting punishment would mean that evil, rather than God, has the last word. If God is to be victorious, hell must be destroyed. As long as hell is permitted to exist, even though it should be in a dormant state, the fact of its existence would be a continual evidence that the divine conquest was not complete.

The prime reason for belief in hell is that God's love is not to be equated with permissiveness—that love is meaningless without justice. It is also suggested that the Father of our Lord Jesus Christ redeems men and that man, by his own choice, gravitates toward hell. Finally, it is argued that a God who saves all men, regardless of their choice, is not loving at all. Such a deity would be guilty of manipulation for His own ends. This would destroy completely man's concept of God as love.

Where hell is a part of the evangelistic proclamation of the church, there is often greater visible success and stronger church loyalty. Whether this measure of success is legitimate and whether this loyalty is valid depends on what one thinks about the level of motivation involved. If the motivation is an appeal to fear, it is so low as to be invalid. On the other hand, if the motivation can lead to a higher level where love for God is more pronounced than fear of Him, the method may be quite necessary in reaching some who must be confronted at the point where they are existing at the moment. A contemporary writer asks, "Are we remiss in not using this immediate fear-dominated age in which to bring home to the conscience the final absolutes, the dread alternative, and the ultimate destinies in the Christian message?" (Ralph Turnbull, *The Preacher's Heritage,* p. 104).

It is our considered judgment that the concept of hell is a legitimate facet of the many-sided gem of evangelism. It must always be kept in balance with the love of God and the freedom of man. To threaten men with hell is not good motivation, but to warn men of the serious nature of sin and its ultimate consequences is probably a logical and needed part of the gospel message. The Good News cannot be fully grasped or appreciated until one has been confronted with the bad news of sin and the inevitable consequences of its mastery. One does not know how to really appreciate what God has done until he is conscious of what the alternative for him would have been.

Almost unanimously, where the concept of hell is still utilized in evangelism, it relates to final separation from God who is the source of life. Hardly any proclamation which includes hell is a literal interpretation of hell as "fire." It is rather loss—irrevocable loss of all that is good about life in communion with God. Such a forfeiture would be, without question, the worst punishment for any man in any hell.

A contemporary university professor gives a modern twist to this concept of loss and suggests what it will be like.

No thing and no one to be loved, and hence no impulse or desire for aesthetic creativity; no knowledge of the meaning of the word *beauty,* or even if there be such a thing. And as for the singing of "endless hosannas" so feared by some, let there be no concern. The glorious priestly music of Bach, Beethoven, Mozart, Mendelssohn, Verdi, and others in their thousands will never once disrupt the gloomy silence, or the noisy din, of the dolorous regions, nor any melody of man or bird mar an eternity of self-loathing.—CALVIN LINTON, *Christianity Today*, November 20, 1970

The above description, though it does not utilize the Biblical terms, is in perfect agreement with the tone set by Jesus in the New Testament.

From the Chair of Preaching in a theological seminary, a professor of homiletics offers the following guidelines for using the concept of *gehenna* in the evangelistic mission of the church today.

1. We must preach hell. This is only fair. It is a fact.
2. We must preach it with tenderness.
3. We must make the New Testament the base of information, especially the teachings of Jesus.
4. We must observe the antithesis of hell—heaven, here and hereafter.

The cults and heretical sects, of course, have a different viewpoint than those of us in the evangelical movement. Their perspective should be known by our ministers and leaders.

There is a sense in which avoidance of hell is an evangelistic appeal. Heaven is a great appeal. Man's depravity was important to Wesley. Christ and Christlikeness is the greatest appeal. Somehow, all these theological factors are intertwined in evangelistic preaching.—DONALD E. DEMARAY

In every presentation of the gospel of Christ the medium through which that word is passed must be faithful to his own prayerfully and studiously concluded stance. That stance must be based squarely upon the Biblical revelation and not upon rationalistic and philosophically oriented data which are foreign or antagonistic to the declared position of sacred Scripture. There is no place to find accurate information except on the pages of holy writ. When the full-orbed Biblical presentation of the gospel is clearly defined and faithfully proclaimed, the resultant evangelistic outcome will be acceptable to all persons to whom the church has been sent and with whom it is called to work.

One of the great Bible expositors of a half-century ago was Lewis Sperry Chafer. His comment is well worth considering as this study is brought to a close. With prophetic insight Chafer writes,

> Men are pleased to receive the Bible revelation concerning Heaven, but do not heed its warning regarding hell. Human sentiment, opinion, and reasons are valueless concerning these eternal issues. It is wisdom to heed the voice of the Son of God, and He more than any other has stressed the woes of the lost (Matt. 5:22, 29, 30; 10:28; 18:9; 23:15, 33; Mark 9:43, 47; Luke 12:5). If eternal punishment cannot be comprehended, it should be remembered that infinite holiness and the sin by which infinite holiness is outraged are equally unmeasurable by the human mind. God is not revealed as one who causes good people to suffer in hell; but He is revealed as one who at infinite cost has wrought to the end that sinners, believing in Christ, may not perish, but have everlasting life.—*Major Bible Themes*, pp. 298, 299

The only conclusion at which we can arrive in view of the limited study to which we have exposed ourselves in this book is that there is a hell. *It is clearly taught in the Bible.* While the fire, worms, dark, and gnashing of teeth may be metaphors for something far more terrible, there can be no mistaking the conviction of both Jesus and His Ancient Church—hell was presented as everlasting punishment. *No man is so good that he can escape hell on his own merits. And no man is so bad that he has no chance.* Men are not destined to hell because of their sins but solely because they do not accept Christ as Saviour and Lord. Not all men will be saved but all could be *if they would only receive the Son of God by faith.*

Let every Christian pastor, church school teacher, evangelist, missionary, church member see his role as one who is sent forth to tell the whole truth—not just part of it—to the whole world. And let us do it with urgency and compassion. The Kingdom *is* coming and we want as many within its realm as will be saved. Even so, Amen!

Discussion Questions for Chapter 9

1. *Summarize the arguments against the doctrine of hell as ever-lasting punishment.*
2. *Reconsider the reasons for belief in a hell which is yet future, terrible, and endless.*
3. *What can be said for the increased visible success in churches where everlasting hell is proclaimed as the end of an unredeemed life? What can be said against such success?*
4. *Is the motivation to fear any less legitimate when applied to hell than when attached to nuclear war or pollution? Explain.*
5. *Can there be any valid good news about ultimate concerns unless there is also a contrasting alternative bad news?*
6. *What does "fire" mean when used of hell in the Bible? What about "worms"? Could these be symbolic and yet hell itself be real in a literal sense?*
7. *Need any man go to hell? How can he avoid it? Is there more than one way?*

10

If I Go to Hell . . . .
(A Sermon)

If your hand does wrong, cut it off. Better live forever with one hand than be thrown into the unquenchable fires of hell with two! If your foot carries you toward evil, cut it off! Better be lame and live forever than have two feet that carry you to hell. And if your eye is sinful, gouge it out! Better enter the Kingdom of God half blind than to have two eyes and see the fires of hell, where the worm never dies, and the fire never goes out. . . .   Mark 9:43–48 LB

Preachers of the Word of God will agree that the hardest and most distasteful theme about which we are called upon to speak is that of final judgment and everlasting hell. It is so much easier to deal with the subject of heaven—though even that is slighted today—than with that of hell. Almost any topic is to be preferred. And this is often the weakness in topical preaching as compared to expository sermons. In a regular, systematic, week-by-week-through-the-Bible exposition of Scripture the faithful pastor or evangelist will eventually be forced to deal with *gehenna* (the Greek word for hell in the New Testament). Preaching on topics will usually allow the preacher to be more subjectively selective. No amount of unpleasantness, however, should permit the Biblical note of hell to go unheard.

The preacher of a full gospel does not create hell nor does he consign any person to its realm. He simply "tells it like it is" as he honestly interprets the living Word of God in relation to the place and its occupants. Each listener must make up his own mind as to whether the presentation has been scriptural and as to what relation it has had to his own life. The quickest way in the world to put the Biblical warning in a bad light and turn people away from giving an open hearing to the ancient Word is done by proclaiming the message of judgment upon sin with an attitude of judgmental delight. Horace Greeley is said to have refused to make a contribution to a religious group who solicited funds to be used in "keeping people out of hell." His reason was that there are not nearly enough people going to hell now! What he may have meant we cannot be certain, but it sounds suspiciously as though he took pleasure at the thought of some people he knew having to suffer forever. No Christian can ever share this kind of bitter, malicious, vengeful attitude toward another. The alarm must be sounded in love.

Has the Doctrine of Hell Lost Its Popularity?

Jesus spoke often about the penalty for sin. Sin brings its reward here and hereafter. At least eleven times He is recorded as having used the word *gehenna* in His ministry. It is likely that He employed the word on numerous occasions of which we have no mention and that on others He talked about the bitter end of sin without actually using the word for hell. To the wicked city of Capernaum He said, ". . . though highly honored, [you] shall go down to hell! For if the marvelous miracles I did in you had been done in Sodom, it would still be here today. Truly, Sodom will be better off at the Judgment Day than you" (Matthew 11:23, 24, Luke 10:15 LB). To the Twelve the Lord gave warning, "Don't be afraid of those who can kill only your bodies—but can't touch your souls! Fear only God who can destroy both soul and body in hell" (Matthew 10:28 LB, Luke 12:5). In the text chosen for this message Jesus uses the strongest possible language to describe the horrors of going to hell.

The word *hell* is the English translation of the Greek *gehenna* which refers to the Valley of Hinnom outside the city walls of Jerusalem where the garbage was dumped and burned. It was to this horrible place that the Lord compared the final abode of the wicked. Hell is God's dumping ground, the place outside the New Jerusalem where all that is unfit for the heavenly community will be discarded. It is an awful picture. Jesus meant it to be. If anyone knew the reality of hell it was He who suffered hell for us on the cross. He literally bore the full penalty for man's sin and thus knew what unredeemed man was destined for in eternity.

The church is always swinging between two extremes. This seems to be the nature of the visible church not yet made perfect. The Puritans appealed almost entirely to man's fear of a holy and righteous God. Man was perpetually "held over the fires" and infants "a span long" were consigned to the pits. Modern churchmen have reacted to the severity of an earlier generation and altogether discarded the concept of fearfulness in the presence of God. God is presented as a loving Spirit who would not hurt a fly! Divine sovereignty is a thing of the past for today's God actually has very little backbone and makes no absolute demands.

> He's a Good Fellow,
> And 'twill all be well.

If hell is mentioned at all it is usually associated with unpleasantness of a mild kind and is considered in a trivial manner. An example is the anecdote about a young lady who was contemplating her forthcoming marriage to an atheist. She explained to her mother that he neither believed in God nor in hell. Her mother assured her that she need not worry since, once they were married, though the mother-in-law might not coerce him to believe in God, she would convince him that there is a hell! Not once did Jesus talk about hell in such a way. There is far more to hell than any earthly degree of unpleasantness. On every occasion when He spoke about hell the Lord was dead serious.

But the modern mind-set is offended by serious talk about eternal punishment on sin. Even church people prefer pastors who will not deal with the fundamental Biblical teachings which disturb their composure. We prefer a pastor like Pope's "soft Dean" described as one "who never mentions Hell to ears polite." Theological schools feel that they are called upon to discredit the teaching of Jesus. The pulpit tones down its message so as to not upset anyone. No alarm is heard in the land because the concept of hell has been challenged by those who find it more comfortable to deny it than to confront it. Thus the general climate within the church and the world is one in which all talk of hell has been abandoned. Even the topic is taboo among people of good taste.

Is Popularity the Criterion for Judging Truth?

Every period of history has had its aversion to revealed truth. Adam and Eve did not want to believe what had been told to them by their Creator. The corrupt people of Noah's time refused to accept the prophetic warning of a coming flood. The Pharisees were not inclined to believe Christ anymore than the earlier Hebrews were disposed to listen to the prophets. Jesus Christ was Truth Incarnate, the eternal Word dwelling in human flesh. In Him God had come down to us, had gotten with us in our plight. The word of law and prophecy was now living and acting right in the midst of the nation of Israel and there was no possible way to miss the divine accent in the life and teachings of Jesus of Nazareth. Yet the churchmen so completely rejected God's complete and perfect revelation of Himself that the Truth was done to death upon a cross.

It has been the oft-repeated story of history that man has determined to live by his wits rather than by God's wisdom. He has rebelled against revealed truth in his frantic struggle to create a system of human truth which better suits him. At no time known to mankind has the human creature been more prone to disbelieve the absolutes of the Bible than during the past half century. We have dedicated ourselves to making the world comfortable and Biblical revelation insists that there can be no lasting satisfaction in a world contaminated by sinful nature. Judgment may well be at our door at this very moment, but no one will dare to believe it. Though our human paradise is filled with dying things which we have planted we continue blindly to prune and water a decaying way of life.

False living demands false axioms. It is much easier to form our axioms on the basis of the way we want to live than to live in accord with divine laws revealed from ancient times by God Himself. How we do enjoy our sins! Anything so pleasant cannot be wrong and if it is not wrong there can be no penalty. So why worry about hell? Man acts as though he is the center of the universe and that everything has been given to him so that he may enjoy one grand fling at the expense of the Creator. Judgment is ignored if not downright denied. Its edge is dulled because we have lessened the severity of sin. Life is amoral, nothing is good or bad *per se,* hence there is no judgment.

We soothe our minds with the fact of divine love. If He is really a God of love then He will not punish us. He is so sentimental that His eyes see sin as only a little naughtiness. Nothing will come of it. Thus we reason without ever stopping to note the law of returns which is indelibly written into the fabric of life. Today has been conditioned by yesterday and tomorrow will be the product of today. "Whatever a man sows, that he will also reap" (Galatians 6:7 RSV). We reap the same thing which we have sown except in greater quantity. How foolish to expect to live a life of abandonment to selfish pursuits and expect to reap anything but tragedy. And if life has any meaning at all, the reaping continues forever.

Many years ago a fine pastor in northern Kentucky picked up a young hitchhiker. They had not gone far until the conversation turned to religion and the boy admitted his careless way of life and excused it on the assumption that there is no hell anyway. No amount of persuasion seemed to change the boy's mind. When they finally reached the juncture of highways where the young man wished to get out, the car stopped and the pastor said, "You may go on living as though there is no hell. I will go on living as though there is. When we get to the end of the way we will both know. If there is no hell I will be as well off as you. But if there is a hell, you will be in trouble. Either way, the man who believes in hell and lives accordingly cannot lose." That is irrefutable logic but there is more to it than that by far.

Jesus assured us that life is not a gamble. Man is moving in one of two ways and each has a definite destination. There is no risk about the outcome. He made that perfectly clear. There are just some ways of living which will prove man's undoing for all eternity. A life of selfishness, disobedience, moral cowardliness, and human self-sufficiency will inevitably lead to final doom. There is no way to avoid that fact.

Must a Healthy Religion Have a Concept of Hell?

To emphasize the physical aspects of hell, except in the manner of symbolism, is to be led down a blind alley. It is true that Jesus referred to *fire, worms,* and *gnashing of teeth.* These images were metaphors, however, which described something far worse. The people understood the pain of being burned and the horror of being eaten by vermin. They could imagine what it would be like to live in a huddle where everybody viciously sought to devour one another. The physical symbols clarified the misery of hell in a way no spirit words could have possibly done. Jesus was using images with which the people were familiar to describe something about which they knew nothing.

When John talks about heaven and depicts it as a place with gold streets, pearly gates, and gem-studded walls it is apparent that he is using the finest of earth to illustrate the glories of a world where all these things are so plentiful as to be commonplace. No one but a miser could be attracted to a heaven where the streets are actually gold! And the physical torment of hell as described by the metaphors used by Jesus is the least of our worries. There is no question but that Jesus meant for us to take Him seriously but to recognize the word picture as a symbolic portrayal of what we could not otherwise understand.

If the fire, the worms, the dark, and the gnashing of teeth do not comprise the horrors of hell, what does? If a man chooses the wrong road and disregards God and Christ and the Bible in his daily living, what will be the consequences? If he never falls at the feet of Jesus and accepts Him by faith as Lord and Saviour, what can he expect?

In the first place, he may count on his life being a witness against him. The record of man's life is being kept in heaven. On that day the books which record man's deeds will be opened. But the one thing which will give irrefutable evidence will be "the book of life" which records the names of those who have come to God in Christ. ". . . if anyone's name was not found written in the book of life, he was thrown into the lake of fire" (Revelation 20:15 RSV). My conscience will no longer be deadened by repeated rebellion but will be keenly alert to accuse me. Either I will have shared in the resurrected life with Christ or I will have lived in such a way as to be guilty of His death. Shakespeare's Richard III says,

> My conscience hath a thousand several tongues,
> And every tongue brings in a several tale,
> And every tale condemns me for a villain.
> Perjury, perjury in the high'st degree:
> Murder stern murder in the dirs't degree;
> All several sins, all us'd in each degree,
> Throng to the bar, crying all "Guilty! guilty!"

I will have no one to blame in hell but myself. Here I may hide behind some churchman whom I consider to be a hypocrite. The excuses which one manufactures here will be of no avail there. They will all burst like bubbles and the hypocrite will not conceal us. Every man carries his passport with him. He has made his choice prior to his death and the event of physical death is nothing more than the transition which brings about the end of his decision.

In the second place, if a man goes to hell he will discover that the most fierce flame to which one can be subjected is that of a burning memory, a memory alive to haunt him forever. He will remember that there is a God who created and preserved him throughout all his days of rebellion. The remorse will be more than he can bear. He will remember that God sent His own Son to die for his sins, that he did not need to come to that place of misery and death. He will remember that it was not what he did or failed to do which sealed his destiny. Every sin can be forgiven save one. Not to have received the redeeming Christ will be to forfeit one's hope for all eternity.

Further, he will remember that the Holy Spirit was faithful to woo him, to prompt and convict him, to guide him to the Saviour. This moment will haunt his memory because even now the Holy Spirit makes his plea. He will remember his neglect of the Bible, his excuses for not being regular in his place of worship, the ministers and friends who prayed for his conversion, and the many opportunities inside and outside the walls of the church structure which he did not use in service to God.

In the third place, the loss which no man can bear will be accentuated by the vision of what he has missed. The rich man in torment saw Lazarus in the bosom of Abraham, a place of final joy and peace. There is no reference to Lazarus's having seen into the realm of the lost. The state of the redeemed will be enhanced because ". . . the former things are passed away" (Revelation 21:4). Those in heaven will not remember those whom they have known but who were lost. But the state of the lost will be doubly hard because the vision of paradise will be open to them without the hope of being there. The joyous festivities, the divine fellowship, the regained paradise will be clearly envisioned.

The unbearable loss will be accented by the ineffectiveness of prayer and the hopelessness of one's condition. Undoubtedly, men will pray in hell who have never prayed before. The rich man referred to above lost no time in getting to the business of prayer. But hell is not purgatory and no prayers are answered in that place. Hell is final and personalities cannot be altered once they are in the grip of that world of no return. Here one can change his home if he does not like his neighbors, the environment, or the climate. But not there! Eternity is forever.

Conclusion

It will be hell to stand at the end of one's days and to know that the landscape he has painted is all gray. Some will do just that. But to stop here would be to act as though Jesus never lived or died. He came that we ". . . might have life and have it more abundantly" (John 10:10). No man need be lost. It is not God's will that any person should ever perish. He offers us life now and eternal life then. The road to heaven is well lighted and there are road signs all along the way for those who are willing to look for them. Furthermore, the side roads which lead into the broad way of destruction are clearly marked lest one inadvertently pursue a detour off the way of life.

Most people plan to do something about their sins someday. Even those of us who treat them as though they were only a little naughty and act as though we do not believe in hell, even we subconsciously anticipate preparing ourselves for the moment of truth. The tragic thing about it all is that we keep postponing an act of repentance and faith in Christ as Saviour and Lord. And someday it will be too late. The devil has no objection to our making plans to turn to the Lord as long as we never carry through on them!

Remember the warning of Jesus: "If your hand does wrong . . . if your foot carries you to evil, cut it off. . . . If your eye is sinful, gouge it out! Better enter the Kingdom of God half blind than to have two eyes and see the fires of hell, where the worm never dies, and the fire never goes out"—(Mark 9:43–48 LB). Nothing could be clearer than that. And nothing could be more urgently important than the taking of an honest inventory of ourselves to determine our preparedness for eternity. It may be much nearer than we are willing to believe.

Discussion Questions for Chapter 10

1. What is the primary difference between topical and expository preaching? Why do expository preachers deal with the subject of hell more than topical sermonizers?

2. *The Ancient Church believed that Jesus suffered hell for us on the cross. Can this be explained so that the modern Christian can understand what was meant by his ancestors in the faith?*

3. *In what sense can hell be said to begin in this life and continue in the life to come? Can one's penalty for sinning be confined to one world and not the other?*

4. *Discuss some instances in which ancient and modern man has adjusted his beliefs to fit his life. Also discuss some in which he had disciplined his life to fit revealed truth.*

5. *Can man be sure of his destiny? What is the secret? If he is not certain, is he in danger? Could he be in danger even though he feels sure of himself?*

6. *Who will be ultimately responsible when a man finds himself in hell? Will such a fate be the result of something one does or something he fails to do? Illustrate your answer.*

7. *What part will memory play in the penalty of sin in eternity?*

Bibliography

Altizer, Thomas J. J. *The Gospel of Christian Atheism.* Philadelphia: Westminster Press, 1966.

The Apocrypha and Pseudipigrapha of the Old Testament, vol. 2, edited by R. H. Charles. Oxford: The Clarendon Press, 1913.

"The Apocrypha," *The Complete Bible: An American Translation,* translated by Edgar J. Goodspeed. Chicago: University of Chicago Press, 1939.

The Apocryphal New Testament, translated by Montague Rhodes James. Oxford: The Clarendon Press, 1953.

Aquinas, Thomas. *The Summa Theologica.* London: Burns, Oates and Washbourne, Ltd., 1922.

Barclay, William. *The Apostles' Creed for Everyman.* New York: Harper & Row, Publishers, 1967.

Barnhouse, Donald. *Genesis—A Devotional Exposition.* Grand Rapids: Zondervan Publishing House, 1970.

Barrett, G. W., and Casserly, J. V. L. *Dialogue on Destiny.* Greenwich: Seabury Press, 1955.

Barth, Karl. *Church Dogmatics.* Translated by G. T. Thomson. New York: Charles Scribner's Sons, 1955.

Barton, Bruce. *The Man Nobody Knows.* Indianapolis: Bobbs-Merrill Co., Inc., 1925.

Berdyaev, Nicolas. *The Destiny of Man.* Translated by Natalie Duddington. London: Geoffrey Bles, Ltd., 1937.

Betts, G. M. *The Beliefs of 700 Ministers.* New York: Abingdon Press, 1929.

Bloesch, Donald. *The Crisis of Piety.* Grand Rapids: Wm. B. Eerdmans Publishing Co., 1968.

119

Bonnell, John Sutherland. *Heaven and Hell*. Nashville: Abingdon Press, 1956.

Brown, Harold O. J. *The Protest of a Troubled Protestant*. New Rochelle, New York: Arlington House, 1969.

Brunner, Emil. *Eternal Hope*. Philadelphia: Westminster Press, 1954.

———. *The Christian Doctrine of the Church, Faith, and the Consummation*. Translated by David Cairns. Philadelphia: Westminster Press, 1960.

Buchanan, Paul. *The Leader and Individual Motivation*. New York: Association Press, 1962.

Buis, Harry. *The Doctrine of Eternal Punishment*. Grand Rapids: Baker Book House, 1957.

Bultmann, Rudolph, and Five Critics. *Kerygma and Myth*. Translated by Hans Werner Bartsch. New York: Harper & Row, Publishers, 1961.

———. *Theology of the New Testament*. Translated by Kendrick Grobel. New York: Charles Scribner's Sons, 1951.

Buttrick, George. *Parables of Jesus*. New York: Harper and Brothers, 1928.

Cadbury, J. Henry. *Immortality and Resurrection*. Edited by Krister Stendahl. New York: The Macmillan Company, 1965.

Cassels, Louis. *The Real Jesus*. Garden City: Doubleday & Co., Inc., 1968.

Chafer, Lewis Sperry. *Major Bible Themes*. Grand Rapids: Zondervan Publishing House, 1926.

Dante, Alighieri. *Inferno*. Translated by Henry Francis Cary. New York: Pollard and Moss, 1885.

Davis, T. *Endless Suffering Not a Doctrine of Scripture*. London: n.p., 1867.

Dodd, C. H. *The Parables of the Kingdom*. New York: Charles Scribner's Sons, 1961.

Dunnington, Lewis L. *Power to Become*. New York: The Macmillan Company, 1956.

Ebbutt, A. J. *Who Do Men Say That I Am?* Philadelphia: Westminster Press, 1957.

Edersheim, Alfred. *The Life and Times of Jesus the Messiah*. Grand Rapids: Wm. B. Eerdmans Publishing Co., 1967.

Edge, Findley B. *A Quest for Vitality in Religion*. Nashville: Broadman Press, 1963.

Edwards, Jonathan. *The Distinguishing Marks of a Work of the Spirit of God in the Works of President Edwards.* New York: n.p., 1843.

———. *The Works of President Edwards.* Leeds, England: Edward Baines, 1807.

Ellicott's Commentary on the Whole Bible. Edited by John Ellicott. Grand Rapids: Zondervan Publishing House, 1959.

Farrer, Austin. *Saving Belief.* London: Hodder & Stoughton, Ltd., 1964.

Gibbon, Ernest. *The Decline and Fall of the Roman Empire.* New York: The Macmillan Company, 1914.

Gleason, Robert W. *The World to Come.* New York: Sheed and Ward, 1958.

Graham, Billy. *World Aflame.* Garden City: Doubleday & Co., Inc., 1965.

Gregory of Nyssa. "The Great Catechetical Oration of Gregory of Nyssa," *Gregory of Nyssa.* Edited by James Herbert Snawley. London: Cambridge University Press, 1956.

Grubb, Norman. *C. T. Studd.* Atlantic City, New Jersey: Worldwide Prayer Movement, 1935.

Harkness, Georgia. *Beliefs That Count.* Nashville: The Graded Press, 1961.

Hancock, Harry N. *And After This?* New York: Longman's, Green and Co., 1954.

Henry, Carl F. H. *Evangelicals at the Brink of Crisis.* Waco: Word Books, 1967.

Hobbs, Herschel H. *Fundamentals of Our Faith.* Nashville: Broadman Press, 1960.

———. *What Baptists Believe.* Nashville: Broadman Press, 1964.

Hobhouse, Stephen. *A Discourse on the Life to Come.* London: Independent Press, 1954.

———. *Selected Mystical Writings of William Law.* London: Rockliff, n.p., 1949.

Hobson, R. F. *Hell.* London: Guild of Pastoral Psychology, 1957.

Hocking, Silas K. *Is There a Hell? A Symposium by Leaders of Religious Thought.* New York: Funk and Wagnalls, n.d.

Hunter, A. M. *Interpreting the Parables.* Philadelphia: Westminster Press, 1960.

Huxley, Aldous. *Time Must Have a Stop.* New York: Harper and Brothers, 1944.

Irenaeus. *Against the Heresies, The Ante-Nicene Fathers,* vol. 1, edited by Alexander Roberts and James Donaldson. New York: Christian Literature Publishing Co., 1885.

Jauncey, James H. *Science Returns to God.* Grand Rapids: Zondervan Publishing House, 1971.

Jeremias, Joachim. *The Message of the Parables of Jesus.* New York: Charles Scribner's Sons, 1963.

Josephus, Flavius. *Antiquities, The Life and Works of Flavius Josephus.* Translated by William Whiston. Philadelphia: John C. Winston Co.

Leckie, J. H. *The World to Come and Final Destiny.* Edinburgh: T. and T. Clark, 1918.

Lewis, C. S. *The Great Divorce.* New York: The Macmillan Company, 1946.

Lindsell, Harold. *An Evangelical Theology of Missions.* Grand Rapids: Zondervan Publishing House, 1970.

Martin, Hugh. *The Parables of the Gospels.* London: SCM Press, 1937.

Martyr, Justin. *Justin Martyr's Dialogue with Trypho,* translated by Richard P. C. Hanson. London: Lutterworth Press, 1963.

Miller, Randolph. *The Clue to Christian Education.* New York: Charles Scribner's Sons, 1950.

Motyer, J. A. *After Death.* Philadelphia: Westminster Press, 1965.

Niles, D. T. *The Preacher's Task and the Stone of Stumbling.* New York: Harper & Row, Publishers, 1958.

Oursler, Will. *Protestant Power and the Coming Revolution.* Garden City: Doubleday & Co., Inc., 1971.

Pannenberg, Wolfhart. *Jesus, God and Man.* Translated by Lewis L. Wilkins and Duane A. Priebe. Philadelphia: Westminster Press, 1968.

Panneton, Georges. *Heaven or Hell.* Westminster, Maryland: Newman Press, 1965.

Paterson-Smyth, J. *The Gospel of the Hereafter.* New York: Fleming H. Revell Co., 1910.

Pery, Andre. *The Heidelberg Catechism with Commentary.* Translated by Allen O. Miller. Boston: United Church Press, 1963.

Pink, Arthur W. *Eternal Punishment.* Swengel, Pennsylvania: Bible Truth Depot, 1951.

Quick, Oliver Chase. *Doctrines of the Creed.* New York: Charles Scribner's Sons, 1938.

Redding, David. *The Parables He Told.* New York: Harper & Row, Publishers, 1967.

Sangster, William. *Questions People Ask About Religion.* Nashville: Abingdon Press, 1959.

Schleiermacher, Friedrich. *The Christian Faith.* Translated in the Second Germanic Edition. Edited by H. R. Mackintosh and J. S. Stewart. Edinburgh: T. and T. Clark, 1928.

Seiss, J. A. *The Apocalypse.* Grand Rapids: Zondervan Publishing House, n.d.

Smith, C. Ryder. *The Bible Doctrine of the Hereafter.* London: Epworth Press, 1958.

Sockman, Ralph. *How to Believe.* Garden City, New York: Doubleday & Company, Inc., 1953.

Stewart, Randall. *American Literature and Christian Doctrine.* Baton Rouge: Louisiana State University Press, 1958.

Stott, John R. W. *Basic Christianity.* Downers Grove, Illinois: Inter-Varsity Press, 1971.

Swedenborg, Emanuel. *Heaven and Its Wonders and Hell.* New York: Swedenborg Foundation, 1952.

Tatian. *An Address to the Greeks,* translated by J. E. Ryland, *The Ante-Nicene Fathers,* vol. 2, edited by Alexander Roberts and James Donaldson. Grand Rapids: Wm. B. Eerdmans, 1951.

The Wesleyan Bible Commentary. Edited by Ralph Earle. Grand Rapids: Wm. B. Eerdmans, 1967.

Thielicke, Helmut. *The Waiting Father.* New York: Harper & Row, Publishers, 1959.

Tillich, Paul. *Systematic Theology.* Chicago: University of Chicago Press, 1957.

Torrey, R. A. *The Higher Criticism and the New Theology.* New York: Gospel Publishing House, 1911.

Tsanoff, Radoslav. *The Problem of Immortality.* New York: The Macmillan Company, 1924.

Turnbull, Ralph. *The Preacher's Heritage, Task, and Resources.* Grand Rapids: Baker Book House, 1968.

Unger, Merrill F. *Introductory Guide to the Old Testament.* Grand Rapids: Zondervan Publishing House, 1957.

Walker, Alan. *A Ringing Call to Mission.* Nashville: Abingdon Press, 1966.

Walker, D. P. *The Decline of Hell.* Chicago: University of Chicago Press, 1964.

Ward, William B. *After Death, What?* Richmond: John Knox Press, 1965.

Watts, Isaac. *The World to Come.* Chicago: Moody Press, 1954.

Weatherhead, Leslie. *The Christian Agnostic*. Nashville: Abingdon Press, 1965.

————. *After Death*. London: James Clark and Co., Ltd., 1923.

Wesley, John. *The Works of the Rev. John Wesley, M.A.* Edited by Thomas Jackson. London: n.p., 1829–31.

What Is Hell? (a compilation). New York: Harper and Brothers, 1930.

Wood, A. Skevington. *Evangelism—Its Theology and Practice*. Grand Rapids: Zondervan Publishing House, 1966.

Index

Abraham   67, 94, 116
Adventists   50
Ahaz, King   17
Aionios   45
Altizer, Thomas J.   92
Ambrose   37
Ancient Church   22, 56, 107
Angels, fallen   17
Annihilation   13, 38, 49-53, 104
Annihilationists. *See* Condition-
    alists
Apocalypse of Peter   32
Apocryphal writings   18, 32, 76
Aquinas, Thomas   32, 37, 69, 75
Athanasian Creed   37
Atonement   47
Augsburg Confession   37
Augustine   32, 37

Barclay, William   58
Barnhouse, Donald   68
Barrett, G. W.   71
Barth, Karl   56
Barton, Bruce   65
Baruch   18
Berdyaev, Nicolas   53
Betts, G. M.   85
Bible concept of hell   12, 13, 17,
    19, 31, 32, 47, 56
Bloesch, Donald   81
Bodiless animation. *See* Inter-
    mediate state
Bonnell, John S.   92
"Book of Life"   115
Brown, Harold O.   70, 89, 95
Brunner, Emil   56, 93
Buchanan, Paul   80
Buddhism   62
Bultmann, Rudolph   23, 24
Bunyan, John   37
Bushnell, Horace   38, 41, 42
Buttrick, George   61

Cadbury, J. Henry   78
Calvin, John   37, 41
Carey, William   76
Cassels, Louis   66
Casserley, J. V. L.   71
Celsus   55
Chafer, Lewis Sperry   107
Chardin, Teilhard de   23
Chauncy, Charles   38
"Child of hell"   21
Choice of heaven or hell   69, 70,
    71, 88, 89, 98, 115-117
Chrysostom, John   37
Conditionalists   51, 53
Conscience   115
Copernicus   22-24
Cosmology   22-26
Curtis, George E.   91

Dale, Robert   38
Dante   29, 31, 34, 35, 37, 44, 69
Davis, T.   65
Death after life   29
Delitzsch, Franz   38
Demaray, Donald E.   106
Determinism   85
Determinists   86
Devillier, Ron   30, 31
Discussion questions. *See* Ques-
    tions for discussion
Divine justice   33, 57, 59, 65-72,
    79, 86
Divine love   58, 59, 65-72, 89,
    104, 113
Divine wrath   82, 104
Dodd, C. H.   44
Drummond, Henry   38
Dunnington, Lewis   88

Early Church   32, 76
Ebbutt, A. J.   67
Edersheim, Alfred   57

Edge, F. B.   80, 95
Edwards, Jonathan   37, 46, 47, 75, 81
Ellicott, John   66
Emerson, Ralph Waldo   61
Enoch   18, 44
Environment, small influence of 86
Erigena, Scotus   55
Escapists   30
Eschatology   13, 77, 78
Eternal self of transcendentalism 61
Evangelism
    as forgotten concept   85-100
    motivation in   75-83, 104, 105, 106
    purpose of   76-78
    urgency as motivation for   77
Existential   36, 53, 77

Farrer, Austin   60
Francis of Assisi   44
Freedom of choice   69, 70, 71, 88, 89, 98, 115
Fundamentalist   12, 86

Garvie, Alfred   38
Gehenna   13, 17, 19, 26, 42, 44, 45, 48, 58, 65, 70, 76, 81, 82, 87, 90, 94, 106, 109, 110
Gibbon, Ernest   41
Gleason, Robert   69, 85, 86
"Going through hell"   30
Graham, Billy   37, 67, 68, 72, 82, 97
Greeley, Horace   110
Gregory Nazianzen   55
Gregory of Nyssa   55
Grubb, Norman   82

Hades   17, 22, 58, 98
Hancock, H. N.   98
Harkness, Georgia   92
Haystack Prayer Meeting   76

Heaven   35, 114
Heidelberg Catechism   70
Hell
    definitions of   29-38
    description of   18, 92-95, 114
    essence of   103-108
    everlasting   37-48, 94
    fear of   41, 46, 78-81, 105
    in New Testament   19, 31, 32, 47, 56, 57, 60, 66, 69, 106, 107
    in Old Testament   17, 31, 67
    interpretations of   29-38, 92-95
    scarcity of writings on   103
    unpopularity of doctrine of 110-114
    word study of   17-26
"Hell on earth"   30, 31
Heredity, influence of   86
Hindu belief in reincarnation   62
Hinnom   17, 110
Hobbes, Thomas   38
Hobbs, Herschel H.   96
Hobhouse, Stephen   37, 61
Hugel, von Baron   46
Humanism   88
Humanitarianism   85
Hunter, A. M.   45
Huxley, Aldous   36, 52
Hypocrite   115

Immortality, conditional, theory of. *See* Annihilation, theory of
Intermediate state   56
Irenaeus   50, 75

Jauncey, James H.   25
Jehovah's Witnesses   50
Jeremiah   17
Jeremias, Joachim   91
Jerome   55
Jesus' teachings on hell   13, 19-22, 26, 36, 59, 66, 88, 93, 94, 100, 110, 114, 117

Jones, E. Stanley   99
Josephus   18
Josiah, King   18
Judson Adoniram   76

Kant, Immanuel   38
Kennedy, James   89

"Lake of fire"   19, 44
Law, William   56
Lazarus   60, 97, 98, 116
Lewis, C. S.   71
Life after death   29
Linton, Calvin   106
Livingstone, David   76
Locke, John   38
Lombard, Peter   32, 37
Luther, Martin   37, 59

Macdonald, George   71
Malachi   55
Manasseh, King   17
Martyr, Justin   50
McLuhan, Marshall   81
Melville, Herman   52
Memory in hell   115
Michelangelo   76
Mill, John Stuart   65
Miller, Randolph   95
Milton, John   18, 37
Moloch   17
Moody, Dwight L.   37
Motyer, A.   93
Munger, Robert   89

Nations, separations of   93
Neander, Johann   38
New Testament   19
Niles, D. T.   77

Orchard, W. E.   36
Origen   38, 55
Ouranos   35
Oursler, Will   12, 13

Panneton, Georges   87, 92
Paterson-Smyth, J.   57
Pauline epistles   19, 56
Pery, Andre   70
Pharisees and location of hell   21, 112
Philo   43
Pike, James   12, 13, 23
Pink, Arthur   87
Platonists   49
Punishment
   everlasting, theory of   37-48, 68, 104
   remedial   55
Purgatory   50, 51, 56, 59-61, 116
Puritans   99, 111

Questions for discussion   14
   chapter 1   26
   chapter 2   38
   chapter 3   48
   chapter 4   53
   chapter 5   63
   chapter 6   72
   chapter 7   83
   chapter 8   100
   chapter 9   108
   chapter 10   117
Quick, Oliver C.   51

Realists   30
Rebellion, 18th century   41
Redding, David   98
Redemption after death   60
Reincarnation   53, 56-62
Remorse   36, 115, 116
Repentance after death   60
Revelation, Book of   17, 19, 44
Ritschl, Albert   38
Robinson, John   23
Rothe, Richard   38
Rubens's painting of *Last Judgment*   32

Sadism   32, 41, 42, 67, 75, 99
Sangster, William   88
Sartre, Jean Paul   36
Satan   55, 66, 99
Savonarola, Jerome   37
Schleiermacher, Friedrich   38, 56
Second chance. *See* Universalism
Seiss, J. A.   33
Separation after death   93, 97, 98
Sermon on the Mount   20
Sermon, sample   14
Sheol   17, 58
Smith, C. Ryder   94
Sockman, Ralph   61
Spurgeon, Charles H.   37
Stoics   86
Stott, John R. W.   97
Sunday, Billy   37
Symbolism   31, 32, 96, 107, 114
Synoptic gospels   19, 44
Swedenborg   31, 34, 71

Tartarus   17, 43
Tatian   50
Tennyson, Alfred   38, 56
Tertullian   37, 75
Thielicke, Helmut   96

"Three-decker" theory   22, 26
Tillich, Paul   50, 56
Topeth   17
Torcello Cathedral   32
Torrey, R. A.   45
Transcendentalism   61
Transmigration   62
Tsanoff, Radoslav   69, 71
Turnbull, Ralph   99, 105

Unger, Merrill F.   25, 94
Universal Flame of transcendentalism   61
Universalism
  proponents and opponents of   38, 55, 56, 87-89
  theory of   38, 55-62, 78, 104

Walker, Alan   77
Walker, D. P.   52, 94
Watts, Isaac   43, 77
Weatherhead, Leslie   38, 59, 87
Wesley, John   37, 43, 44
Whatley, Richard   38
Whitefield, George   37
Wish-Fulfillment   29, 52
World Council of Churches   82
Wyclif, John   37

DATE DUE

JAN 9 1974	JUN 1 8 1983		
OCT 12 1974	1983	APR 1 3 2006	
MAR 1 9 1975	DEC 2 1 DEC 1 0 1984	NOV 2 2 2005	
JAN 7 1976	MAR 7 1985	NOV 2 4 2009	
JAN 2 2 1976	1986 I I DEC 5 1986		
FEB 4 1976	APR		
DEC 1 6 1976	NOV 1 7 1986		
MAR 1 5 1977	DEC 1		
DEC 2 0 1977	DEC 1 5 1986		
	NOV 1 6 1988		
AUG 1 6 1979	DEC 1 4 1988		
DEC 4 1979	MAY 3 0 1990		
APR 3 1980			
DEC 8 1980	NOV 0 2 1995		
DEC 2 0 1980	NOV 2 1 1995		
APR 1 2 1981	MAR 0 9 1998		
APR 3 0 1982	MAR 2 3 19		
DEC 2 1 1983	MAR 0 6 2000		
GAYLORD			PRINTED IN U.S.A.